ADVANCE PRAISE

"Will Leach has done a great job with his first book, Marketing to Mindstates. He's taken what could be a complex topic and really simplified it into an easy-to-read and understandable format. Additionally, he gives great examples of how you can apply his process to your own brands that are very actionable. Definitely worth the read."

—REGAN EBERT, SENIOR VICE PRESIDENT OF MARKETING, DR PEPPER SNAPPLE GROUP

"Marketing to Mindstates is an amazing secret weapon for any marketer or business leader looking to understand their consumers better or gain an edge in driving actionable insights to transform their strategy. Will has such a gift for taking supercomplex theory and his years of experience and breaking it down into accessible concepts that made it simple to understand and implement in my own business. Highly recommended!"

—MICHAEL MESSERSMITH, GENERAL MANAGER, OATLY

"Will Leach is a passionate man, a deep thinker, and has a mind that constantly moves at 100 mph. All of this is present in his book, Marketing to Mindstates. Yet, what really comes through is the clarity with which he talks about the behavioral sciences in the context of everyday marketing and how all of us can apply his model in both marketing and research. The book is full of fascinating examples, clear ideas for implementation, and yes, passion for the subject matter. Every marketer and researcher should have this on their bedside table."

—SIMON CHADWICK, MANAGING PARTNER, CAMBIAR CONSULTING

"This book is really engaging and relatable, especially to those of us who have worked in consumer/shopper insights. As a fellow student of behavioral science, I know this stuff can be overwhelming and a challenge to make sense of. Will has done an impressive job of making sense of behavioral design and saving the rest of us from having to go through the effort to get there on our own."

—PHIL MCGEE, PRESIDENT, DECISION BREAKERS, AND HOST OF SHOPPERNOMICS PODCAST

"I highly recommend Marketing to Mindstates to anybody who wants to apply behavioral science to improve their marketing. Not only is Marketing to Mindstates a thorough science-based book, but Leach's Mindstate Activation Model is communicated in a clear, approachable way, making these *concepts very actionable for anybody to use. If the goal of the book is to be a 'practical guide' to applying behavior design to research and marketing, that goal has been reached."*

—ERIC SINGLER, GLOBAL CEO, BVA NUDGE UNIT

MARKETING
TO
MINDSTATES

THE PRACTICAL GUIDE TO APPLYING BEHAVIORAL
DESIGN TO RESEARCH AND MARKETING

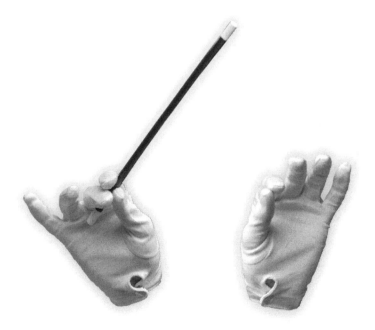

WILL LEACH

LIONCREST
PUBLISHING

MARKETING TO MINDSTATES

*The Practical Guide to Applying Behavior
Design to Research and Marketing*

ISBN   978-1-5445-1240-2 *Paperback*
       978-1-5445-1241-9 *Ebook*
       978-1-5445-2095-7 *Audiobook*

This book is for those who don't give a damn about behavioral science and really just want to design better marketing that gets people to listen, care, and act.

CONTENTS

INTRODUCTION

It was the morning of June 17, 2009, in Frisco, Texas, when I made the most shocking realization of my professional life: almost everything I'd learned over my entire consumer marketing career up to that point was simply *wrong*.

And not just a little wrong, either. I was grossly mistaken about *everything*. Here's the scary part: you, and likely every marketer you know, are not actually sure why some of your marketing creative works and why some of it doesn't. As an industry, we are shooting in the dark because we don't understand how to message to people's subconscious minds.

I don't say this to shame you—in fact, just the opposite! I say this to inspire you. You can be more intentional with your marketing by applying the principles of behavioral science, which will result in much more consistent success in your creative. And I'll show you how in this book.

But back to that June morning.

How can I pinpoint the date of my realization so precisely? Easy—that's the morning my wife, Melanie, gave birth to our beautiful baby boy.

One of the first important decisions Melanie and I had to make when we found out she was pregnant was which day care to choose for Nicholas. The amount of anxiety you feel when another parent asks you where you'll send your child is excruciating. You always feel like it's a setup—a way for other parents to rank you by how much you love your soon-to-be child. Because of these societal pressures, you will spend literally months trying to find the perfect day care (and, as you may know, getting the day care right is no laughing matter when your wife is seven months pregnant and nesting).

Now, I'm what I refer to as a "pros-versus-cons" junkie, which played a huge role in selecting a day care. Ever since I was a little kid, I've loved collecting data and comparing everything. I've been this way my entire life, so there's no point fighting it now. It's just a matter of working with it.

In fact, it was my own childhood that turned me on to this

method of decision-making. My fifth-grade teacher, Ms. Peeler, once said that if it was done right, a pros-and-cons list would make all of my choices fast and easy. It struck me as magic. In order to make the best decision possible, all I had to do was list out every pro and con I could think of for the different options, place them on separate sides of a list, and calculate which side had the most points.

And I love this method. I've used a highly organized comparison of pros and cons to help me make the most important decisions in my life. Should I join the U.S. army? What college should I go to? Should I stay with my girlfriend? (Sorry, Bess.) Should I take this job?

Pros and cons are my oracle, and I am a devoted disciple.

When it was time to find the perfect day care for our new son, Nicholas, I once again turned to my rational, structured approach. Four months before Nicholas was born, Melanie and I started seriously scoping out local day-care centers. We asked friends at work and in the area for recommendations and started narrowing candidates.

After we'd visited our top seven, I created my exhaustive list of pros and cons to select three finalists. From there, we planned to meet with each of the finalists for a final round of interviews and evaluations, choose the one with the most pros, and get placed on their waiting list for the coming year. Easy, right?

When Nicholas actually entered the world, my foolproof, logical plan went right out the window.

Here's what happened on that June 17 morning: Melanie gave birth prematurely with a chorus of nurses, doctors, Aunt Shirley, and beeping bedside equipment welcoming Nicholas into our lives. This should have been the happiest moment of my life, but I'm telling you right now that I was an absolute wreck, both emotionally and physically. I knew deep down that I wasn't prepared to take home a baby in a few days.

When we first drove to the hospital, we were expecting only a short precautionary trip—a pat on the back, a nice fat bill, and a drive home to go on with our lives. But that's not how life works. I was supposed to have another five weeks to prepare our house and my mind for our son. Hell, I hadn't even installed the car seat yet.

Melanie could see the desperation in my eyes, even several hours after she'd given birth. She told me to go home, pick up a few hours of sleep, and come back with the baby bag we'd prepared at the house (but didn't bring to the hospital the night before).

I was off to complete my first "dad" task as a new father. Big pressure.

I don't remember much about my walk to the parking lot, except for muttering something to my wife's Aunt Shirley. It was all a blur. I was a brand-new father, and I could only feel the rush of pure joy, love, and frankly, inadequacy that comes with having your first baby. I was low on sleep and even lower on ideas of how to be a responsible, loving dad. With that heavy weight on my shoulders and a strong desire to start off my new role right, I left the hospital.

And that's when I saw it.

On my way out of the parking lot, just as I pulled onto the street, I noticed the sign for one of our finalist day-care centers, Carpe Diem. I knew I was tasked with another duty—go home and get some sleep—but I pulled into their property on adrenaline and instinct.

When I walked in, the look on the receptionist's face said it all. She had seen new fathers in my mindstate hundreds of times before. I barely had to open my mouth to tell her my story—all about our premature son, my wife having no idea she was about to give birth, the rush of doctors and nurses in the delivery room—before she put her hand up to quiet me.

She smiled and said, "You don't have to go any further. I get it. We're nearly full, but we have exactly one spot left for the Fall. It's yours if you want it."

Right there, in a moment of panicked excitement without my wife, I signed up on the spot. I made the spontaneous decision without so much as a second thought, let alone a full-on pros-and-cons list. It was *incredibly* uncharacteristic of me, especially for such an important decision. My temporary emotions took over and I acted on them.

I acted spontaneously. And you know something? It felt good. *Really* good. I didn't need a list to tell me the right thing to do, and I didn't need a reason or permission to do it. I just felt intuitively that I was behaving in the best interests of my newborn son, even though I didn't use my logical mind to make the decision.

It worked out fine in the end. Carpe Diem took great care of Nicholas. But still, how could this happen? How could I possibly ignore four months of painstaking comparisons and randomly choose one finalist to take care of our son? I can rationalize it after the fact as the act of a loving father—and that *is* part of the explanation—but how do you explain why any of us go against our best-laid plans and act on pure instinct and emotion?

Why do we act contrary to plans, or against logic in general?

Why do we buy things that we know we don't need?

Why do we make the same bad choices again and again, even when we know we'll feel worse in the long run?

And most importantly for you, how can marketers tap into this behavioral phenomenon to deliver messaging and experiences that consumers *truly* want?

These are simple questions, but it turns out that the answers aren't simple at all. Don't get me wrong, I felt great about my decision to get Nicholas into Carpe Diem, but the troubling part is that it wasn't fully *my* decision.

In that moment, I was acting on behalf of my subconscious mindstate as a desperate new father, and I wasn't even aware of it.

MOST OF US AREN'T THINKING AT ALL

That seemingly simple decision to choose a day care without thinking it through gave me a spark of inspiration. It sent me on a journey that spanned years as I researched and tested the wide-ranging wisdom of psychology and behavioral science that had influenced my spontaneous decision.

I began to deeply study human decision-making in earnest while I worked in the Customer Insights Group at Frito-Lay. We spent huge sums of money understanding how psychology and our environments work together to influence our purchase decisions.

Today, nearly eleven years after my son's birth, I have definitive answers as to why we so often buy irrationally. And the answers aren't what you think they are, and they aren't as widely available as I'd like. That's why I'm writing this book.

This is my passion, but it doesn't have to be yours. I've done the work in this field—conducting hundreds of consumer research studies and working with dozens of neuromarketers over twenty years—so you don't have to.

In short, when it comes to buying decisions, most consumers are simply not thinking at all.

HOW IS THIS BOOK DIFFERENT?

In the past twenty years, we've learned more about human decision-making than we did in all the previous years of human history, and the technology is finally catching up to the science and the theory.

We are living in the golden age of behavioral understanding. When you integrate the robust and underutilized science behind consumer behavior with the art and design of marketing, you can emotionally connect with people like never before.

Yet most of us don't give a damn about behavioral sciences. And you know something? That's perfectly OK. In fact, that's exactly why I wrote this book. I love this stuff and have dedicated my work life to deeply understanding it. But I also come from the real world of business where theory is cheap because results matter. I know that the science of behavioral change is too full of jargon and fancy words to be applicable to most. And this has always bugged me.

I wanted to make these seemingly complicated concepts easy, accessible, and finally, applicable for marketing researchers, marketing directors, and marketing creative professionals at any level. I've relentlessly studied psychology, goal theory, motivational psychology, behavioral economics, and neuromarketing to uncover the code to the world's most persuasive marketing. And this code has designed a marketing model that is proven to drive consumer behavior.

To make everything in this book actionable and empowering for you, I've purposely gotten rid of the intimidating jargon and details and focused only on the big, important stuff. The behavioral scientist in me cringes at this decision, but the marketer and entrepreneur part of me knows this is what you actually want and what the broader marketing industry needs.

So, if you are looking for a book on marketing theory, stop reading now. This isn't for you.

At its core, this book is about one thing: understanding and activating the temporary, subconscious mindstates that heavily influence people's receptivity to marketing..

WHAT IS A MINDSTATE?

In short, "mindstates" are activated in temporary moments of high emotional arousal, otherwise known as a hot state.

When we are in an emotionally aroused mindstate, like when I was leaving the hospital, we rely on more subconscious, emotional factors to make decisions, making us more susceptible to influence. That's the underlying reason for why emotional marketing—the kind that I'll teach you in this book—works.

That's just a complicated way to say that you're going to learn how to design marketing creative in a way that speaks to people's emotional mind rather than their rational mind. That kind of marketing gets people to listen, care, and act.

Despite a fancy phrase here and there (always accompanied by a simple explanation), this is *not* a theory book or an academic book.

This is a field guide to using behavioral science to lower psychological resistance to marketing to solve real business problems. The stories, experiments, and insights in this book all come from actual challenges I've faced in my personal life and in business—often with millions of dollars at stake.

WHAT YOU'LL LEARN IN THIS BOOK

In the chapters that follow, you'll be introduced to the powerful Mindstate Behavioral Model. This model, which I developed over the course of decades of testing and research, incorporates four unique social sciences that, when integrated, form a comprehensive understanding of the subconscious factors that drive all human behavior.

Whether you're a marketing researcher who is being asked to justify your budget or a marketing professional being pressured to improve marketing ROI, this book will empower you with basic knowledge, and more importantly, it will provide you with direct, actionable tactics to design marketing creative and experiences that are psychologically more effective, drive an emotional response, and urge your customer to behave differently.

In short, you'll learn how to develop subconscious messaging that compels consumers to *choose* your brand through behavior design. You can also visit my website mindstategroup.com to continue your marketing education.

BEHAVIOR DESIGN

So what is behavior design, you ask? Well, to me, behavior design is the process of applying the latest neurological and behavioral insights to the development of customer interactions to psychologically influence and change consumer behavior. It's the recipe behind today's best marketing—marketing designed to get people to listen, care, and act. We'll talk a lot more about specific behavior-design factors throughout this book, most specifically psychological mindstates.

To that end, this book is broken down into three sections:

1. Understanding the real drivers of consumer behavior
2. The Mindstate Behavioral Model that you'll use to trigger specific mindstates
3. The application of the model to marketing research and advertising creative

Additionally, the appendix contains basic profiles of the eighteen different mindstates so you can apply the

Mindstate Behavioral Model to get the most out of your marketing starting today. But we're getting ahead of ourselves.

First, I'm going to teach you how to deeply understand how your customer behaves and why.

Are you ready to learn how?

PART ONE

UNDERSTANDING HUMAN BEHAVIOR

CHAPTER 1

WHY DO WE DO THE THINGS WE DO?

In 2010, I was a senior manager of marketing research for PepsiCo, working on the brand-marketing initiatives for our SunChips brand. In my position, I got invited to a lot of conferences, most of which I couldn't attend. But on a whim, I chose to attend the Future of Persuasion Conference, mostly because it had a cool name.

I'll be honest: I wasn't expecting much.

However, within the first forty minutes of the keynote speech, I realized that every aspect of marketing and marketing research was going to fundamentally change within the next ten years.

THE FUTURE IS HERE, AND IT'S VUCA

The keynote speaker said that the world is approaching a state of VUCA—Volatile, Uncertain, Complex, and Ambiguous. Technologies are scaling faster than ever, he told us, so we're going to have to adapt quickly, which creates a VUCA world. People would soon be creating content with their smartphones at exponential rates. In this new world of consumer control, we would be inundated with thousands (yes, thousands) of marketing messages every day. In his words, any business would be able to reach any prospect with any message, anywhere, at any time they chose. Keep in mind, in 2010, when this conference took place, digital was becoming more ubiquitous, allowing people to create and access content across all devices, including cell phones, televisions, computers, tablets, and, very soon, watches. And marketers from any company in the world were newly able to reach the same consumer on multiple platforms daily. Marketing was scalable at a global level for any brand, and it was only a matter of time before people would adapt to this new marketing onslaught.

The broader discussion at the conference focused specifically on marketing, all aimed toward answering this question: if the world is changing so dramatically, how will marketing change with it?

The keynote speaker posited an idea that changed my perception of marketing forever:

"As marketers, we have to understand how to hack the most advanced filtering system ever created: the human mind. Because of the impending marketing onslaught, people will psychologically filter out the vast majority of advertising. Technology could help you get through these ever-evolving filters, but it's clear now that it will be challenging."

To find the answers to how we marketers can thrive in a VUCA world, the speaker dove into the area of behavioral science—more specifically, the psychology of persuasion.

Over the course of the presentation, two particular concepts stood out to me:

1. We make a *staggering* number of decisions on a daily basis.
2. In the course of making (or not making) those decisions, we process an equally shocking number of marketing messages.

Let's take a deeper look into these two modern-day realities.

First, our brains are now tasked with making more than 35,000 decisions *per day*. As a result, the vast majority of our decisions must be made at the *subconscious* level.

Our subconscious minds are constantly processing everything happening in our environment, and it adds up to be about a novel's worth of information—*Harry Potter*, for example—every *hour*.

Second, we're now *constantly* bombarded with marketing. These messages come at us from every platform we access and read. We're exposed to thousands of marketing messages each day, each one trying to influence the thousands of decisions we need to make.

As much as it pains me to say, we simply *cannot* take the time to conduct a pros-and-cons list for every one of our 35,000 daily decisions. If we tried to do that, we wouldn't even make it through breakfast before we wanted to jump out a window.

When you combine these two concepts with the reality of VUCA, you come away with the harsh truth for marketers:

1. There is a lot of subconscious noise in consumers' minds.
2. It's only going to get *harder* to break through that noise.

WHY IS THIS HAPPENING?

The world is becoming more VUCA because as we become more connected to our devices, our information platforms will continue expanding rapidly.

Look at it this way: at first, brands thought their ability to inundate consumers in their messaging was a good thing. New social media sites, as well as entirely new media platforms such as Netflix, meant that brands had intimate access to people beyond television, radio, newspapers, and other traditional channels. This was great news, right?

It wasn't. What's happened instead is a complete overwhelming of the consumer.

In addition to smartphones and tablets, consumers can now access media on their watches, their smart TVs, and voice-activated artificial intelligence, such as Alexa, Siri, and Google Home.

When will this media inundation stop? The truth is it's *never* going to stop; it's only going to *increase*. As a result, our psychological filters will become even stronger to survive.

If you are lucky enough to get your marketing to break through that psychological filter, your message *will* be considered by the consumer, and it *will* be more likely to be acted on.

How do you break through the filter? Many marketers get lucky by getting bolder with their activation and messaging. But that's almost always the wrong choice.

BOLDER ISN'T BETTER IN THE LONG RUN

In 2012, the Doritos brand team came up with one of the loudest, boldest marketing campaigns I've ever seen. In an effort to go viral, they set up a fifty-plus-foot vending machine that doubled as a concert stage at South by Southwest Music Festival. It had flashing LED lights and giant bags of Doritos chips, and it featured artists such as Snoop Dogg, Ice Cube, and Public Enemy.

It was incredibly grandiose, and they brought it back several years in a row. And now it seems rudimentary.

Did they get a significant ROI on their incredibly breakthrough marketing campaign? Maybe, maybe not. It's almost irrelevant. Even if successful, that urge to go bolder creates a dangerous cycle for Doritos *and* its competitors.

Think about it like this: after Doritos's giant vending machine stunt, Pringles thinks it has to get even bolder so it can break through the marketing clutter. So it creates a pop-up store in Times Square allowing people to mix and match unique flavors with Al Roker from the *Today Show*. Then Doritos thinks it has to go even bolder, so it responds by making a *hundred*-foot stage at the next year's South by Southwest. You get the point?

Suddenly, something that once seemed grandiose—a

multistory vending machine concert stage—isn't wild or big enough to break through the marketing noise. So you're in an endless cycle of overspending to make a lot of marketing noise. Eventually, you'll run out of money and real estate to keep building giant vending machines.

The endless cycle of one-upping your competition will only get more expensive for everyone as you try to reach consumers on different platforms. It's simply unsustainable financially, particularly in our current corporate environment where CEOs are forcing marketers to justify their jobs by calculating ROI on an almost daily basis.

So you can go viral. OK, so what? What's the ROI on going viral? A million retweets doesn't lead to anything close to a million conversions.

But what if I told you that you can use Mindstate Marketing strategies and tactics in a *subtle* way to get through your consumers' subconscious filter? In this way, you dance your way past it, not smash through it with a sledgehammer.

THE BETTER (BUT LESS OBVIOUS) PATH

After I learned about the VUCA world we were moving toward—where most brands will compete by overspending on building the boldest, most unbelievable brand experiences—I realized that nobody seemed to be thinking about the subconscious filter that prevents marketing messages from actually reaching most consumers' consciousness. I couldn't rationalize overspending to break through this filter when he was telling us that we could instead design marketing to pass through this filter. So that's exactly what I focused on for several years.

Luckily, I worked with visionary leadership and had a massive amount of resources at PepsiCo. I was able to dive headfirst into behavioral psychology and the application of techniques in persuasion—even if it didn't always go according to plan.

THE FUNDAMENTALS OF MARKETING RESEARCH ARE SEVERELY BROKEN

When we conduct advertising research, we often ask consumers what they think about an advertisement and how they will act in the future after engaging with it. The problem is that no matter how hard they try, most people can't explain why they do things with any consistent accuracy. Our research methods are severely broken because of this fact.

Consumers often create rationalizations for past behaviors, developing reasons why they *believe* they did what they did. The truth is, most consumers don't really understand *why* they do what they do. But you can. Most times, behaviors are highly influenced by the context we are in when we make the decision. In fact, there are four unique contextual factors you can harness that greatly affect consumers' decisions even more than their rational minds. Therefore, it's really important for marketing research to truly understand these contextual factors in greater depth when conducting research for brands.

THE FOUR FACTORS OF CONTEXT

The first three factors—location, people, and feelings— are of course important for you to understand. However, the last one—choice architecture—is the most important factor relative to the behavioral marketing model I'm teaching you in this book.

LOCATION, PEOPLE, AND FEELINGS

Location refers to where we are when we make a decision. The way we behave inside a church is very different from the way we behave in a sports stadium. Social norms guide much of our perceptions of acceptable conduct and behavior, and a lot of that is based on where we are at a given moment.

The second factor, people, is who we're with when we're making a decision. When I'm with my young son, Nicholas, I eat very differently than I do when I'm out with friends at a bar. I doubt I'd be clinking beer glasses with my son, but that's exactly what I'd be doing with my friends. We often change our attitudes, beliefs, and preferences based on whom we're with when making a decision.

The third contextual factor is how we're feeling at the moment, both physiologically and psychologically. *Physiologically*, if we're hungry or sleep-deprived, we're going to behave very differently than we would if we were well-fed and well-rested. That's why we're told we shouldn't shop in a grocery store when we're hungry. We'll have even less control over our purchasing decisions than usual in that situation. *Psychologically*, our opinions, beliefs, and actions will be different if we're in love or in a good mood, compared to when we're in a bad mood. We might buy flowers and chocolates when we're in love, or SpaghettiOs and Ben & Jerry's when we're depressed.

CHOICE ARCHITECTURE

This is the most important contextual factor—it's the one you should be most interested in if you are a marketing director or creative professional. Architecting choice refers to *how* choices are presented in the moment of decision.

As a marketer, you can't control someone's location, the

people they're around, or the mood they're in when engaging with your creative, but you *can* control how you frame your message within that creative. You can control the architecture of the words you put in your message, as well as the visuals you include, just like we did with some behavioral experiments at a place called Earl's.

THE TEST GONE WRONG

PepsiCo had an advanced laboratory in Dallas, where, for years, we conducted many different marketing experiments. The laboratory was huge—as large as a big-box store—because its purpose was to replicate an actual shopping environment, but environments that we architected and controlled.

We made it look like a grocery store with ten different aisles, products on the shelves, endcaps, and everything else a grocery store would have. We even had checkout clerks and fake shoppers (people paid to act like they were shopping), to make the environment feel more natural to the seventy-five test consumers we monitored on any given experiment.

One of my most surprising insights came from a test on packaging changes. We'd recruit consumers to shop the store, then flip the store overnight (meaning we updated products with their newly designed packaging), and the next day, we'd bring in a new group of consumers to shop. We'd be looking for a sales lift, seeing whether more people would buy a particular brand on day two, after the products' packaging changed.

Our tests normally went according to plan. Normally.

One night, we were supposed to get a shipment of chips with new packaging designs for a test, but the shipment never came. We'd already run the first day of the experiment, and I'd already recruited the second group of people to come in the next day, so we decided to have the second group shop the same environment as the first group, establishing a bigger base group of shoppers for the experiment.

When we went to aggregate the test results between the two groups, we noticed something odd. Even though they'd shopped in the same environment, there was a *significant* difference between chip sales on the two different days.

In the world of classic marketing research, this should *never* happen. There should not have been any significant difference in purchase behavior between the two groups because nothing had changed among the testing variables. And yet there was.

I controlled the variables. I had the same price points, same packaging, same planogram, same flow, and same types of people. I even did the test during the same time of day.

And yet the two data sets were *dramatically* different when it came to the shoppers' purchase behavior. This wasn't supposed to happen, ever, in marketing research. At least that's how traditional marketing saw it. If two groups of similar people are exposed to the same products, with the same messaging, and the same price points, then they should make similar purchases.

Because that didn't happen, the results of our testing didn't just challenge the survival of our laboratory, but in my eyes it also challenged everything I knew about marketing research.

It was a scary place to be. I was given a clear message from our leadership: you've got to figure out what happened here. Because if we don't, we're going to start reconsidering the massive amount of money we spend each year on this research facility.

So we had to get creative.

WHAT YOU CAN LEARN FROM EARL'S CONVENIENCE STORE IN AUBREY, TEXAS

Our shopping lab was a wonderful resource, but it just

wasn't real life. We had to pre-recruit people to shop in a particular way for the experiments, we had cameras all over the place, and we had five neuroscientists on call at a given moment. I don't know about you, but I've never been to a grocery store or Walmart with even a *single* neuroscientist on call, let alone five. Not to mention it cost PepsiCo about $75,000 just to run a single study.

In the heart of the Great Recession, and after a decision to focus on other priorities, we had nearly our entire research budget and team taken away. All the company's money went to branding and innovation, so we poor souls in shopper research were left to fend for ourselves—just me and my lone partner, Julie.

With our jobs and the entire lab on the line, we had to think outside the box of our department-store-sized lab. We found our answer in an unlikely source: the nearby town of Aubrey, Texas—population 2,500. Prior to my working on improving the lab, Julie scoured the Dallas/Fort Worth metroplex trying to find the perfect store to run small, cheap behavioral studies. And she found the perfect solution in an independently owned convenience store named Earl's.

Julie did the legwork and started to befriend a very sharp but cantankerous store manager at Earl's named...well, let's just call her Cathy. Cathy was not easy to read most days, but she was always willing to listen to ideas that would help her store grow. After a few days of Julie just helping around the store and many hours of listening to Cathy complain about her vendors, Julie was able to convince Cathy to just listen to our proposition to turn her store into a real-world behavioral laboratory. As you can imagine, the initial idea did not go over well with Cathy. But she was open to hearing more, particularly after we offered up some incentives to make it worth her effort. Days later, we went to meet Cathy at Earl's.

"We're from Frito-Lay, and we'd love to do some experiments in your store. We'd just like to come in, make some changes to the messaging on a few products, switch out a few promotional ideas, and collect some data on your customers' behavior. Would you be open to that? We'd pay you, of course."

She gave us both a long, hard look, took a deep breath, and said, "I suppose that'd be fine."

"Excellent!" I said. "Now, what would you like in return? Name your price."

"Well, sir, I've been in need of a new rolling hot dog grill for some time now, so I'll tell you what. If y'all can get me that new hot dog grill for the store here, I'll let you do it. Just tell me what you learn so I can make my sales."

I just about cheered in Earl's little convenience store. Instead of paying $75,000 for an experiment in our previous lab, we had full access to all of the data we could ever want for the low one-time price of a thousand-dollar hot dog roller and some software.

We got her the hot dog roller and put a server in the back office to analyze every sale that came through the register. To run the experiments, we occasionally changed the shelves overnight when no shoppers were in the store. Then, for the following two to four weeks, we'd check out the new sales results.

What were we looking to accomplish?

EXPERIMENT #1: WALK TOWARD THE LIGHT

At about the same time we started working with Earl's, our company started to lose significant penetration of our brands inside of similar convenience stores nationwide. One-dollar-menu deals were becoming a big trend in fast-food chains such as McDonald's, Taco Bell, and Burger King. As a result, people were getting more meals from fast-food restaurants and going to convenience stores less often. To compete with fast-food, convenience stores started offering their own meal deals, such as two hot dogs and a drink for two dollars, or two hot dogs for a dollar. But that meant bad news for us. People were now bypassing the chip aisle in convenience stores in favor of those heartier meal deals.

At Frito-Lay headquarters, our sales team started to ask, "How do we get people to bypass the hot dogs and meal deals and go down the chip aisle instead?"

Most guys who actually work hard for a living are not going to buy a bag of chips for $1.29 when they can get two hot dogs for that same amount of money (or less money, in this case). How could we make the salty snack category relevant for the hungry blue-collar guys who often walk into convenience stores for a low-cost meal, not snacks?

After we discovered these shoppers were simply bypassing our aisle once they saw these massive meal-deal programs near the hot dog/nacho/taquito bar, we knew that we needed to devise a unique, inexpensive way to draw visual attention away from those bars and into our chip aisle.

Like many of my behavioral research projects, I started my work reviewing Google Scholar to see if there were any behavioral science findings we could leverage. In my research, I found a little-known study that revealed a strange human behavior that I thought might be crazy enough to work. People have an avoidant response to blinking lights, such as yellow traffic lights or red hazard lights on a car. These blinking lights can subconsciously create an avoidance response neurologically and psychologically. In layperson's terms, blinking lights piss off our brains.

But this study found that there's an exception to this rule—*white* lights.

For whatever reason, our minds tend to actually *like* blinking white lights. It's a distraction, but a less jarring one, and people often walk *toward* the light instead of away from it. (Hey, kinda like that movie *Poltergeist*!) Because of this odd phenomenon, I decided to spend $65 at a local Kinko's to put a small blinking white light in the signage underneath our chips. But even if we drew shoppers' eyes to notice our chips, how would we break through their psychological filter?

Along with the white lights, we also tailored our messaging to match the psychology for the guys who were coming into Earl's convenience store to buy snacks. I knew two things about this group:

1. Hunger was the number one reason they went to convenience stores at lunchtime.
2. As a result of their desire to optimize and win, they wanted to feel like they got the best deal for their money.

Competition was big for them. Based on our previous research, we knew that these men often used metaphors around competition and battles when talking about their day. These men often said things like, "Man, work is just so difficult *every day*. Every day is a battle, and I simply have to win."

With all of these insights in mind, I created a new shelf strip and put it underneath the Doritos. It was a black shelf strip with white lettering, and all it said was, "Beat hunger with Doritos. Winning never tasted so good." Why these words? I applied what I learned from my studies in psychology and neurology to the actual messaging. Associate my brands with the consumers' desire to win. Science-based design at its best!

Beat was a competition word, so I wanted that. *Hunger* was an important word to use because it was the number one reason they were going to convenience stores. Last, the blinking white light was placed between the two sentences inside the Doritos logo. We installed this shelf strip later that night and waited a week to see the results.

When the results came in, I was over the moon. From this behaviorally designed marketing, we had a 6 percent category sale lift without *any* discount. Traditional marketing research would normally recommend dropping the price or giving something extra to the consumer, but I didn't do any of that.

I simply used behavioral science to drive my creative strategy and tapped into what I believed was driving these shoppers' subconscious mindstate in the moment. Psychologically, the words *Beat hunger with Doritos* were optimized for these guys' mindstate when inside of Earl's convenience store. We used quiet, subtle changes to our message to break through their psychological filter to get into their subconscious mind and speak to their needs more directly, without having to make our message over the top or any louder.

EXPERIMENT #2: DISCOUNTING GUILT

Our next experiment at Earl's sent us in a different direction.

We were looking to address another behavioral problem for PepsiCo—getting people to buy multiple PepsiCo brands in the same purchase. So, once again, I went straight to Google Scholar, but this time, I turned to a different behavioral principle to inform our solution—hedonic bundling.

PepsiCo, which owns Frito-Lay, decided to invest in barrel coolers—the types of coolers you fill with ice and load up with soft drinks and chips, then place near the checkout in convenience stores. This was a way to reach the people who were skipping the soda or chip aisle.

The goal was to deploy these barrel coolers to drive purchases of soda *and* chips in the same trip. To do that, the chips and sodas were bundled together for $2.22, and we made signs to place on top of the coolers to promote this discount. Buy a soda and bag of chips from this cooler, and you can get them both for a discounted price.

But when the promotion was launched across the country, shoppers were *not* buying enough of these discounted bundles to make up for the costs of buying and delivering the barrel coolers to the convenience stores.

At that point, the sales team was once again asking us, "What can we do to make these barrel coolers pay off?" The coolers and refrigeration units had been a big investment.

I approached the problem in a similar way as my previous marketing research experiences. I wanted to understand *how* consumers were making decisions—especially as those decisions related to their subconscious minds—and design messaging from there.

In the traditional concept of bundling, consumers typically get a discount on the *total* bundle of products. If they buy two products together, they save money on *both* products.

However, based on research pulled from my friend Aaron Reid of Sentient, we tried something different. Instead of applying the discount evenly across two items, what if the total discount was applied to *only* the item that they felt most guilty about buying?

This is the concept of hedonic bundling. People get the same discount overall, yet they feel like they're getting a better value than if you discounted both items because you're also reducing their *guilt*.

Suddenly, shoppers make a rationalization for behavior that is driven by their subconscious needs. They say, "You know what? It's not *so* bad for me to buy both the chips and the soda because I'm getting a huge discount on the soda, which is what I really want."

In the original display, Pepsi used very traditional signage placed over the barrel cooler with an image of a Pepsi can and Lay's chips above it with the phrase, "Better Together," which reinforced the idea that we were selling two items together for a discounted total price of $2.22.

Traditional wasn't working, so I worked with Julie and the small local creative agency she worked at to redesign this original signage offer in a way that would increase its effectiveness psychologically. First, we showed a race car crossing a finish line. The race car crew chief had his hands open and arms up in victory, surrounded by a checkered flag. The marketing said, "Fuel up, thirst down, and drive away a winner."

This messaging targeted much more of the action-oriented, achievement-focused motivation we were trying to tap into. These guys wanted to be winners. They wanted to feel like they were winning the battle every day.

So how did we apply the concept of hedonic bundling?

Instead of buying the soda and chips together for $2.22, this offer would allow the customer to buy the chips for full price and *save $0.55 on the soda*. It was the same total discount but now placed entirely on the soda, because our research showed that shoppers felt worse about buying soda than they did about buying chips.

It was that simple, and it worked. When we made those subtle changes, there were weeks we experienced a 20 percent lift in cross-purchases. In our world, that's a *massive* increase.

More importantly, I made a larger realization. *My gosh*, I thought, *we didn't have to explain why these bundles made economic sense, and we didn't have to convince consumers to want our chips. We didn't even have to lower the price. All we had to do was reframe their perceived cost.*

And after these two experiments, my journey to becoming a behavior designer became my full-time occupation. I would commit my life to doing this full time. I resigned from Frito-Lay a few months later to start my first company, TriggerPoint.

TO DO BEFORE MOVING ON

- Understand that VUCA is very real and is highly influential in consumer behavior. Consumer decisions are exponentially more complex than they were just five years ago. Ask yourself, "How does VUCA impact our customers' behaviors now and in the future?" If you don't know, get help from someone who does.

- Identify how context (e.g., location, people, and feelings) impacts people in the moment of decision. Always conduct behavioral research in a *real* context where people make *real* decisions. As the saying goes, "If you don't understand the context, then you don't really understand your consumers."

- Leverage behavioral-science-based research methods to understand the true drivers of behavior. Traditional "question and answer" marketing research would have told me to lower prices to drive topline growth. Behavioral science research, on the other hand, told me to tap into achievement motivations and discount guilt.

- Before conducting new consumer research, search Google Scholar (scholar.google.com) for the latest academic research on that problem you're trying to solve. There's no reason to always reinvent the wheel and you'd be surprised how much you can learn from brilliant academics across the globe.

- Once you understand these behavioral insights and know people's unspoken desires, don't let that knowledge go to waste. Apply it directly to your marketing strategy and executions—primarily in subtle ways. And again, if you don't know how, get help from a behavior marketer who does.

- Visit my website mindstategroup.com for more tips and resources.

CHAPTER 2

WHERE MARKETING AND RESEARCH FALL SHORT

Traditional marketing research practices are predicated on flawed perceptions of the human mind. As marketers, we like to think of the mind as a pristine well full of wants, needs, and desires that are clear and well thought out. We assume we can drop a bucket into that well (for example, asking people *what they think* about an idea), bring it up for examination, and investigate people's reactions. Then, using the insights we gleaned from our investigation, we build a billion-dollar business and retire—or at least get promoted.

Here's the problem: the human mind isn't a pristine well. It's a *muddy pit*.

Behavioral science makes it clear that consumers don't actually know very often why they do what they do, but luckily, the era of behavioral enlightenment is now underway. Thanks to new research and technology in the areas of neuroscience and behavioral psychology, we now know more than ever about how people really make decisions. Despite the fact that we are only *beginning* to understand why people do what they do, we *do* know that the human mind utilizes two different systems to make everyday decisions.

What are these systems and how do they work?

SYSTEM 1 AND SYSTEM 2

We'll refer to these two decision-making systems as System 1 and System 2.

System 1 automatically and subconsciously recognizes patterns to form initial judgments to facilitate easier decision-making. This system creates biased actions very quickly and without much consideration.

System 1 is often described as your subconscious auto-pilot, and it's influenced by your current situational contexts as well as your emotional mindstate in the moment. When you utilize your System 1, you're not engaging in strong, conscious cognitive thinking. You're just reacting.

Most importantly, the System 1 part of your brain underpins *every* decision you make, even those big rational life decisions such as choosing a college, buying a house, or selecting a day-care center for your first child. You can't turn off System 1. System 1 is *always* running in the background—reacting to the environment and processing information, even against your will.

Because it governs the majority of our decisions, System 1 is the more powerful and influential of the two systems. I like to think of it this way: System 1 is one of the massive server rooms at Google, constantly processing information at millions of bits per second. Then, when it's done processing a certain piece of information, its output is mainly *how you should feel.*

System 2, on the other hand, is the rational, pros-versus-cons list mind. It's more like an old Commodore 64 computer, processing information at about fifty bits per second. It's not that the Commodore 64 doesn't work; it's just slower, clunkier, and a bit prone to mistakes. It can't handle the same amount of information as the Google server room. That would be overwhelming. Instead, it processes smaller amounts of information, and its main output is *what you should do.*

My point is we don't think nearly as much as we *think* we do. We are *not* rational beings influenced by emotion. Instead, we are *emotional* beings who hope to *rationalize* our behaviors after we make them. We're kind of funny that way.

Because System 1 is constantly working—and is naturally more emotion-driven—emotional mindstates ARE the driving force in human behavior. And to understand these subconscious mindstates, we need to understand the four key factors they're made of—your consumer's goals, motivations, regulatory approach, and the cognitive heuristics they use when making decisions.

THE SUNCHIPS BIO BAG DISASTER

In 2011, I was managing consumer insights for the Sun-Chips brand. As one of the first chip brands made with whole grains, we spent years positioned as a healthy snack brand, and we did well in that space. However, that year we made the decision to reposition SunChips as an environmental brand to add to the wellness portfolio at PepsiCo.

We thought we could appeal to the rational part of our

customers' minds—their System 2—with an environmentally friendly compostable bag (which, for this story, we'll simply refer to as the bio bag). We spent millions of dollars designing and creating advertising for the launch of our new SunChips bio bag, which was specifically designed to help eliminate waste by decomposing quickly in composters. We were on the hook for running commercials, print ads, and out-of-home campaigns and had sold the new packaging to every major retailer in the country. We were all-in.

Then, a few weeks before the launch of our new bag, I got a call from the brand manager.

"Will," she said, "you need to come to my cube and see this bag. It's going to *kill* us."

"I'll be right there," I said, hanging up the phone. I thought she was just overreacting to something small just before a huge product launch. Whatever she had to show me couldn't be nearly as bad as she made it sound, right?

Boy, I was dead wrong.

I walked into the hallway beside her cubicle, where she lined up two of the bio bags on top of her filing cabinet.

"Look at this bag," she said, holding it up.

It had a very glossy finish. "That's really cool," I said. "I haven't seen one of these bags in person before."

"Grab the bag," she said, as she pointed at it firmly.

The moment my hand touched it, the bag crackled so loudly it sounded like glass shattering. (I swear, literally glass shattering was what I heard.)

Nevertheless, I tried to remain optimistic. "Well, I don't know how big of a deal that is," I said. "I mean, it scared me a *little* bit, but it's going to be fine. And our brand lovers say that they *want* bio bags. They don't want to pollute the environment. They want a brand with a real purpose. They'll show us some grace."

We had mere weeks before we'd launch these compostable bags for every flavor of SunChips across the country. We had factories already churning out thousands of rolls of packaging film. We'd even run an ad on *American Idol*. We couldn't back out now.

The brand manager handed me the two prototype bags and asked me to test the impact of the design. I grabbed both of them and speed-walked back to my office.

I immediately emailed my team for help in finding a party. Luckily, our administrative assistant, Laura, was having some friends over that weekend. "Take this bag of chips to the party," I told her, "and put it on the table with all the other snacks. Don't open the bag. Just watch people interact with it and let me know what happens."

With the second bag of chips, I immediately went to the local Kroger grocery store and made a beeline for the chip aisle. I replaced the first SunChips bag I saw with the prototype bio bag, then stood nearby with my shopping cart, waiting as I pretended to shop for chips. After what seemed like days, another shopper stopped at the SunChips and reached her hand out to grab the bio bag.

I will never forget what happened next.

She grabbed the bag, and it emitted its unbelievably loud shattering noise. She jerked her hand back from the bio bag like it had exploded. It *scared* her. My God, it actually scared her! She carefully moved the bio bag out of the way and chose the bag of SunChips behind it.

We're in trouble, I thought. *We're in a lot of trouble.*

On the following Monday, I asked Laura what had happened with the bag of chips she took to her party. "Well," she said sheepishly, "the bag *was* the talk of the party. But it was because nobody would touch it. A few people actually asked what was wrong with the bag."

Here's a fundamental law of marketing: don't scare people with your product. Unfortunately, it was too late to really do anything about it, so we decided to launch anyway. The bag was a disaster. Sales dropped quickly, and retailers noticed. We had YouTubers holding decibel readers up to the bag. People called our company to tell us that we triggered epileptic seizures because of the bag. Customers refused to eat the chips at work because of how loud the bag was. It became the butt of memes across the internet. And none of our previous packaging research saw it coming. Why?

Because we thought we could override people's emotional System 1 minds and appeal to their logical System 2 minds. No amount of environmental friendliness could get people to overlook the feeling that this bag didn't feel or sound right.

People told us they wanted a compostable bag; they said it was the right thing for the environment. However, their logical System 2 desires didn't account for the emotional decision that they'd make at the actual party, grocery store, or even in their office.

Our customers' motivations mattered *a lot*. It's just that we didn't understand what they were. Despite what they said, our customers cared less about saving the environment than they did about being stared at each time they reached into our bag. Our misunderstanding of their true subconscious motivations changed everything for the SunChips bio bag. In fact, within a matter of months, the packaging was discontinued.

But that damn YouTube video remains. You should look it up!

Source: theblaze.com

EMOTIONAL MARKETING

Temporary mindstates—such as the moment you hear a shockingly loud chip bag—can override natural preferences, beliefs, and values. They can lead consumers to make decisions that go against their stated intentions.

This is why you may find yourself getting a bit out of control when you're in Las Vegas. It's not because you've changed your belief systems; it's because you're in a temporary mindstate that modifies, or even disregards, those beliefs while you're under its power.

Vegas casinos actively work to overstimulate you to activate these mindstates. And they do this better than almost anyone. Imagine you're inside a windowless building with no clocks, tons of flashing lights, people cheering, and the ding-ding-dings of slot machines going off every few seconds. Your brain can't help but try to process every stimulus it encounters, but your mind quickly becomes overwhelmed. Moreover, you're sleep-deprived, you're likely drinking, and your sense of time is completely out of whack. It's much more difficult to control your spending and gambling in that environment. Instead of limiting yourself to the hundred dollars you planned to gamble with, you suddenly find yourself withdrawing a *thousand* dollars, completely out of control. You act off adrenaline and emotion rather than reason.

SALAD OR CHEESEBURGER?

How we eat is another common arena where our mindstates influence our behaviors. I used to compete in Ironman triathlons. Now I wake up every Monday and think, *Will, you do not look like a triathlete anymore. You have to eat better. You've got to do something different this week.*

No problem. Without hesitation, I start the week by eating healthy. In fact, eating healthy shouldn't ever be a problem for me, because I actually *do* like salad. I'm not kidding! I *do* want salad on most days, and on Mondays, I'll normally eat that salad.

However, by Wednesday, I run into trouble. I might be having a rough week at work. My wife, who's from Cajun country, might make red beans and rice on Wednesday night. Not a big deal, but it's definitely not salad. Then on Friday, I go off the rails, eating a double cheeseburger at Five Guys and drinking beer at the Thirsty Growler.

Why does that happen? It's not because I prefer Five Guys over salad. I actually prefer salads over cheeseburgers. But here's the thing. *We don't think as much as we think we think.* More often than not, we don't actively think at all when we make our food choices. We react. As the week goes on, my willpower diminishes, so I become more susceptible to messaging that keys into my emotional mindstate. Therefore, on Fridays, I feel emotionally drawn toward a certain choice (like, oh I don't know, a cheeseburger) and tell myself that I prefer it to eating a salad today.

If a survey asked me what I prefer to eat, I'd say that I prefer a salad.

But what do I actually eat?

I eat cheeseburgers.

Simply put, our preferences aren't as stable as we'd like to think, because they are influenced by our in-the-moment mindstate.

BE AN EARLY ADOPTER—OR DIE

Psychologically speaking, we all want to make our lives easier.

Life is volatile. It's uncertain. It's complex. It's ambiguous. And all of this drives how we make decisions—consciously and subconsciously.

Because we make so many decisions every day, and we're inundated with so many marketing messages, we often seek the path of least resistance without even realizing it. The easiest decisions are the most fluid decisions. And the most fluid decisions are the ones driven by the subconscious, System 1 mind—decisions where you don't feel the need to do a pros-and-cons analysis. These are decisions that feel natural and intuitive because your heart and gut are telling you to do it.

As consumers, we don't *want* to be influenced by an irrational state of mind, but we are, and as time goes on, more and more companies are going to try to tap into that System 1. If in five years you're still appealing to consumers' System 2 brain—focused on only explaining the benefits of your products—then you'll be left in the dust.

Recent research found that companies that apply behavioral economics outperform their peers by 85 percent in sales growth and more than 25 percent in gross margin.

You have an opportunity in front of you: you can be an early adopter before most companies realize the world of marketing is changing.

If the Carpe Diem day-care center would have been a five-minute drive down the tollway, one exit away, I would *not* have gone there and signed up. My job at that moment was to go home, get a nap, and pick up our baby bag.

But I was in a new mindstate. I now had a strong desire to be an achiever as a new dad. And there was Carpe Diem, right across the street, with the right messaging (seize the day!) and context to meet my needs at the perfect time. That was System 1 thinking at work, and it's a perfect example of how and why we make decisions that feel intuitive and easy.

Carpe Diem was in that location before the hospital; otherwise, I'd give them credit for trying to capitalize on the heightened emotional mindstate of new dads leaving the hospital. But with me, they got lucky. They just happened to be in the right place at the right time.

Getting lucky won't be good enough for you as we go forward. More and more, companies are running experiments and designing their marketing creative to tap into people's subconscious minds. What are you doing?

Right now, most brands aren't sophisticated enough to design marketing to appeal to people's emotional mindstates on a consistent basis. You can be.

TO DO BEFORE MOVING ON

To begin marketing to consumers' mindstates, there's a simple four-step process to follow.

1. Find decision "trigger points."

First, you have to identify *where* people are when they're actually considering and making decisions for your product. These "trigger points" are where people are most susceptible to persuasion, so it's important to understand the environment in these moments. When you place relevant System 1 messaging at these trigger points, you will exponentially increase the effectiveness of your marketing.

Answer these questions in detail: Who is there? Where are they? What is happening? What time of day is it? All of these factors are important in understanding what type of tactics you can and should use.

2. Identify the mindstate.

Next, in those moments of decision-making, identify the key emotional mindstates your customer might be in.

If you understand the subconscious mindstate your consumer is in, it will completely change your messaging. For example, if you know your consumer is in a "Cautious Nurturance" mindstate (which we'll discuss later in the book), then you understand that they're trying to show love for others but in a way that prevents their rejection.

This insight should completely change your marketing strategy. Now, in your messaging, rather than simply saying, "Two dollars off chocolate bars," you can say something more relevant to them, such as, "Show your wife you *care*. Save two dollars on chocolate, and buy her roses."

That's *far* more powerful and effective, and you would have *never* known to do it if you were only looking at traditional marketing research. You would know that a lower price mattered to the consumer, but you wouldn't know *why* or *how* to message to it.

3. Tap into (or activate) the mindstate.

After identifying your consumers' key mindstates, you need to use a mindstate persona and marketing blueprint to design marketing creative that subconsciously taps into these mindstates and influences decision-making. We'll discuss this further throughout the book.

4. When necessary, activate the mindstate you need.

If you can't find these mindstates and trigger points, or if you're not able to reach consumers in an emotionally aroused mindstate, you can actually create them. (God, I love behavioral science!)

Maybe you don't have the budget to do research or just can't figure out how to do it. No problem. You can trigger subconscious mindstates temporarily based on what you intuitively know about your customers.

In many cases, you can temporarily prime a consumer into a mindstate. If the messaging is done right, you can actually make a consumer temporarily feel like an optimistic achiever versus another emotionally charged mindstate.

To accomplish this, however, you *must* understand behavior design.

And that's exactly what we'll cover in the next chapter.

More information about these steps is available at my website mindstategroup.com

CHAPTER 3

WHAT IS BEHAVIOR DESIGN?

One day in January 2016, I got an unsolicited phone call while I was doing a behavioral audit inside a Safeway grocery store in Dallas. It was a North Carolina number I did not recognize. I don't normally answer calls from unknown numbers, but for whatever reason, I answered. And I'm so glad I did. Let me take a moment to summarize the conversation.

"Hi. This is Will," I said.

"Hi, Will. My name is Phil, and I know this is a bit out of the blue, but I typed 'behavior design' into Google and you were one of the top results. I saw you worked for Frito-Lay?"

"That's right."

"That's perfect, because I own a company that indirectly competes with Frito-Lay, Carolina Fine Snacks, and we're going to revolutionize the American diet. We've developed a nutrient-rich salty snack that tastes great and is actually great for you. It's not a healthier snack; it's nutrition in snackable form. It's a game-changer in the industry, and there's nothing in the world like it. But I need help getting it launched. We're a twenty-man operation, and we've never directly marketed snacks. We have no marketing team and no money for advertising. We haven't even sold the idea to any retailers yet. I'm an inventor and definitely not a marketer. But I know one thing for sure: we won't compete with Frito-Lay for long with less than 1 percent of Frito-Lay's marketing budget. And we can't change the American diet if we can't get people to notice or try us. Can you help us?"

What Phil said next absolutely floored me. "We *need* your help, Will. I think the only way to compete with Frito-Lay is by marketing to people using behavior design."

My jaw dropped. Nobody used that term, even in 2016. This small company in Greensboro, North Carolina, knew they had to change the marketing game because they knew they couldn't compete with the juggernaut that is Frito-Lay under the same rules. This realization and the passion in Phil's voice made all the difference on that call. Within two weeks, my creative partners and I boarded a flight to North Carolina to meet the guy who wanted to design a brand from the bottom up using mindstate strategies and behavior design.

From the moment I met Phil in person, I knew we'd made the absolute right choice. He walked me through his factory, which was full of decades-old, decommissioned manufacturing equipment he'd purchased cheaply from other manufacturers to keep his costs down. He favored people over technology and employed a lot of people with various challenges, so he reengineered his equipment and jobs so these employees could work there. He actually used to work for Frito-Lay in the late 1970s, but he was a man who needed to live on his own terms, so he left after only two years and started a company with little more than a belief that he could build something amazing. And he did.

When I talked to Phil and listened to his story, I immediately wanted to make him a billionaire. Of course that wasn't his goal—and it wasn't my plan—but that's how inspiring he was.

"All we have is the vegetable chips themselves. We don't have a name, a logo, a tag line, packaging—nothing. Do you think you can do it, Will? Can you help us?"

"Phil," I said, "I'm not only going to help you, but we're going to create the world's first behaviorally designed brand from the ground up."

In short, by using behavior design, we'd take on this challenge by using advanced behavioral and neurological science to influence consumer behavior. We'd build an entire brand from the ground up that spoke to people's subconscious first—something that had never been done before.

The first thing we did was develop a brand identity and name. We discovered through some basic behavioral research that Phil's target consumers were motivated by independence, so we wanted a name, logo, and tag line that reinforced people's desire to feel autonomous. So, we came up with the name Wicked Crisps and the tag line, "Deliciously Deceptive Nutrition."

Deliciously Deceptive Nutrition

Our target consumer, millennial moms, wanted to have it all; that's why they were eating vegetable chips. They want the nutritional benefits of vegetables without the guilt that comes with snacking on fatty chips. So we emphasized the good versus evil aesthetic. We put a halo over the *i* in "Wicked" and a devil's tail trailing off the *r* in "Crisps."

We then used an oblique orientation on the font of the tag line—meaning it didn't have any strong edges—which biologically drew the eye toward it and psychologically helped create another good-versus-evil contrast with the font of the Wicked Crisps name itself, which was more bold and rebellious.

Then we designed the logo. We wanted to blend two sides of the same person, one for good and one for evil. We even designed the hair to be interwoven to show that it is the same person but with very distinct traits.

Why did we design it that way? Because we wanted our imaging to reflect the same level of autonomy our customers want to feel. They are unique individuals who have distinct—often contradictory—desires swirling inside of them at all times. We wanted to speak to their System 1 mindstate.

Note: If you want to immerse yourself into the entire case study of how we developed the Wicked Crisps brand, visit mindstategroup.com.

DESIGN OF THE TIMES

Previously, I told you that behavior design is the process of applying the latest neurological and behavioral insights to the development of customer interactions, to psychologically influence and change consumer behavior. Want to see how behavior design works in everyday marketing? Try this now:

- Pull out your phone (or any device with an internet browser).
- In your browser or a search engine such as Google. com, type in the word *watches*.
- Click on the image tab.

Do you notice anything similar among all of these watches? Look closely as you scroll down the image list. What do you see?

When I ask this question to most groups, the most common answers are, "They're all circular," or, "I see a logo." But that's not quite it. There's something else that is oddly similar across most watch pictures.

Take a look at the time. If you're like most people, you're now realizing the answer. Nearly all of the watches show the same time: 10:09. Seriously. Go look at Google Images and see for yourself if you don't believe me.

What do you think drives this phenomenon? What makes 10:09 such an important time to display on the vast majority of watch pictures?

There are plenty of theories. Some say it's because the watch hands look like a smiley face at that time. Others say it's because the watch hands frame the brand name or logo to bring attention to it. There's even a theory floating around that it's an homage to President Lincoln because he was shot at that time.

Once I recognized this phenomenon, I had to know the answer. There had to be a reason why every watch company displayed this time. I went to an expert I knew could help me find the answer.

A few years ago, I asked a friend who was the CMO of Zales Jewelers at the time. While we were sitting at lunch, I showed him a recent store catalog for watches that he sold in his stores. I pointed to the watches, all of which displayed the same time: 10:09. He hemmed and hawed and came up with "plausible" reasons until finally admitting to me that he didn't actually know. They'd just always done it that way, and he'd never asked his advertising agency why.

Well, if you are a neuropsychologist, you might have a very interesting perspective on this that will come up later. But first, a short story.

The story begins almost a hundred years ago with a young, curious store clerk trying to sell more watches. The story goes like this:

In the 1920s, a retail clerk for Hamilton Watch Company,

a small manufacturer started in Lancaster, Pennsylvania, in 1892, discovered something amazing. When he set their watches to 10:09 before placing them on display, they sold better.

Word got out that this seemingly magic time helped boost sales. Within a decade, every major watch company displayed their watches at 10:09 for display in stores as well as their advertising.

The ads for the Waltham Watch Company dating from 1930 show watches set to 10:09:36. So do the ads for Timex and Omega (beginning in the 1940s), Chanel and Rolex (1960s and 1970s), and Swatch Watch (in the 1980s). And as you've just seen for yourself, the practice continues today. Hell, just this week I noticed a clock display at Walmart. Want to know the time that was set on every clock? 10:09.

WHY DID SALES GO UP?

What could explain the boost to sales in relation to the watch hand angles?

Well, to my neuropsychologists, the answer could lie in something called cardinal orientation. Cardinal orientation, meaning straight lines and sharp angles, are easier for our eyes to pick up than oblique orientations, or curves. That tendency is built into the biology of our eyes.

You might ask, "What does that have to do with watch sales?"

The answer is simple. Curves actually create greater visual interest *because* they're harder for us to visually pick up.

Imagine this: You're walking by a storefront filled with watches in 1920 and very bad lighting. You happen to look down at the watches on display to check the time, but it requires more than a glance. What would happen if you couldn't quite read the time on the watch? Wouldn't you initially try to look a little harder? Sounds like a trigger point to me.

That's all it can take for an advertiser to get you to stop and pause, and maybe trigger an emotional mindstate that increases interest in a new watch versus someone simply walking by. If I'm a marketer and I scientifically design this to happen, I'm driving attention to a watch that shoppers would've otherwise ignored.

That's the essence of behavior design—understanding the real whys behind behaviors and designing for it. There could be small biological, neurological, or psychological reasons in play, among others.

Behavior design is part intuition, part artistry, and part

science, all merged together to influence the heart and the mind. It doesn't *replace* great marketing creative—it *builds* on it.

INTUITION IS NO LONGER ENOUGH

Today, veteran marketing directors and creatives still base many creative strategies solely on intuition. But presenting those decisions with the justification that they're informed by "decades of experience" is no longer enough to gain trust from a client. Marketers today are under increasing pressure to justify their marketing by ROI. Under these conditions, hope and experience just aren't enough. The clients are going to reply with, "Well, that's just your intuition. Tell me *specifically* why this strategy is going to work."

It's an understandable question from the client. When millions of dollars are at stake, operating on intuition alone is a scary proposition. Clients want more than intuition.

And we can't just keep saying that we must experiment to learn and therefore A|B test it. Half of marketing budgets seem to be spent doing experimental A|B testing to find a solution. At some point marketing directors are going to wise up and stop spending one-third of their marketing budgets on marketing experiments.

Behavior design can drive a more concrete conversation about creative solutions. Clients are more apt to trust creative solutions based on neurological and scientific concepts they can understand—concepts such as cognitive bias, regulatory fit, and other scientific factors that we're going to talk about throughout this book.

If you were a brand investing $5 million on a Super Bowl ad, which of these two statements would you rather hear from your agency creatives?

- "You know, we just feel that it's important to have a group of young people interacting with the product."
- "We'd recommend having a group of young people interacting with the product to tap into the belonging motivation and the science of social proof."

Easy choice, right?

Not only does the second choice sound better, but it *is* better. It's got science behind it. That's what behavior design does, and a statement like that gives you ammunition to go with your gut. In other words, you can validate your instinct-driven ideas with the support of behavior-driven science.

BEHAVIOR DESIGN IN ACTION

Behavior design triggers emotional mindstates—those moments in a consumer's engagement or shopping journey when they're in higher states of emotional arousal and most susceptible to emotional decision-making and influence.

To maximize the effectiveness of your marketing to consumers, you'll need to find or create these mindstates. To do that, you'll need to understand and execute using the four behavior factors below to increase the levels of persuasion of your marketing and drive more sales for your company.

BENEFITS OF BEHAVIOR DESIGN

Everyone benefits from behavior design and marketing to mindstates—consumers, retailers, and marketers. How?

1. More sales. Creating emotional mindstates can increase persuasion and buying momentum for your products.[1] Retailers also benefit because emotionally aroused shoppers buy more products in general.
2. Fewer returns. Shoppers in emotional mindstates

---

1   Forster, Higgins, and Idson, "Approach and avoidance strength during goal attainment: Regulatory focus and the 'goal looms larger' effect," *Journal of Personality and Social Psychology*, 1998.

make happier, more confident buying decisions.[2] They're less likely to return products or feel buyer's remorse.

3. Higher satisfaction and repeat business. Shoppers have more enjoyable experiences in environments that have been psychologically or behaviorally designed.[3] Those environments feel better and more natural to consumers and drive more repeat visits.

4. More engagement. Consumers feel an increased understanding of your product.[4] If you design a product that naturally taps into consumers' subconscious, they feel like they understand the product more.

People who understand your product will *engage* more with it. And the more people engage with your product, the more features they'll likely experience. The more features they experience, the more they'll like your product and tell others.

Consider a smartphone buyer who uses it for little more than a phone, ignoring many of the apps on the device. They'll miss out on everything else a smartphone can

---

2 Idson, Liberman, and Higgins, "Distinguishing Gains from Nonlosses and Losses from Nongains: A Regulatory Focus perspective on Hedonic Intensity," *Journal of Experimental Social Psychology*, 2000.

3 Ibredi and Higgins, "Shoppers Have More Enjoyable Experiences," 1996.

4 Higgins, "The 'self digest': self-knowledge serving self-regulatory functions," *Journal of Personality and Social Psychology*, 1996.

do and not see much value in it, compared to an old flip phone.

But if some behavior designer were to psychologically optimize the experience of buying and using that smartphone, the buyer would be more likely to play around with it and use the apps. They'd engage with more features, experience more benefits, and feel a higher perceived value of the product.[5]

Why is that important? Because it means they'll literally pay *more* for your product or service (yes, behavior design can increase profitable topline growth for your brands).

Research by E. Tory Higgins also shows that advertising that has been behaviorally designed improves the results of advertising in five ways:

1. Increased marketing "breakthrough" (breaks through the clutter)
2. Longer engagement with the advertising
3. Increased understanding of your message
4. Increased memorability of your message and brand
5. Increased trust and believability of your message and brand

---

5   Idson and Higgins, "How current feedback and chronic effectiveness influence motivation: everything to gain versus everything to lose," *European Journal of Social Psychology*, 2000.

WICKED CRISPS AND THE FOUR BEHAVIOR FACTORS

For Wicked Crisps, our intentional use of behavior design in the snack name, the tag line, and the brand imaging helped us become one of the hottest snack brands around—getting placed in 20,000 retail stores—without *any* traditional marketing.

That's the power of behavior design. You can build more effective marketing creative that is built on science *and* art, not just guesswork. Phil and I used behavioral research to identify our target's goals and motivations to specifically create a brand that tapped into their subconscious mindstate to influence behavior.

THE FOUR BEHAVIOR FACTORS

1. Goals: What is the job to be done for the consumer?
2. Motivations: What is propelling your consumers to go after their goal?
3. Regulatory approach: How do consumers approach their goal?
4. Cognitive heuristics: What mental shortcuts do your consumers use to make their decisions easier?

These four factors drive most consumer behaviors and decisions, and we'll cover them in further detail in the following chapters.

When you build marketing around all four factors and you trigger those emotionally aroused mindstates, you're also creating much more effective marketing. They're the key building blocks of creating subconscious emotional arousal. I'm going to show you how these factors can be specifically used to identify mindstates and how to message to these mindstates to make your marketing more effective.

THE MINDSTATES

As I mentioned in Chapter 2, consumers are often influenced by one of eighteen different mindstates when they're making decisions. Your strategies and tactics need to be *specifically designed* for these mindstates (you can find persona profiles for each mindstate in the appendix).

THE EIGHTEEN MINDSTATES

1. Optimistic Achievement
2. Optimistic Autonomy
3. Optimistic Belonging
4. Optimistic Competence
5. Optimistic Empowerment
6. Optimistic Engagement
7. Optimistic Esteem
8. Optimistic Nurturance
9. Optimistic Security

10. Cautious Achievement

11. Cautious Autonomy

12. Cautious Belonging

13. Cautious Competence

14. Cautious Empowerment

15. Cautious Engagement

16. Cautious Esteem

17. Cautious Nurturance

18. Cautious Security

Again, if you don't know your consumer's mindstate or you don't align your marketing creative correctly with it, you risk losing *everything.* Your messaging is going to feel off to your consumers, and they're going to decide—consciously or subconsciously—to ignore your brand and choose your competitor instead.

So how do you determine the key decision-making mindstates of your consumers?

ENTER THE MODEL

After years of research and testing across numerous industries, I've developed the Mindstate Behavioral Model to help marketers determine the key decision-making mindstates of their consumers.

Using this model, you'll ultimately be able to identify specific personas to design for and create strategy-driving *behavior design blueprints* to guide your creative. You'll have an effective, science-based strategy and specific tactics that can be used to *influence* consumers' receptivity to your messaging and your brand.

YOUR NEXT STEPS

The first stage of this powerful model is to identify and define each of the four key behavioral factors we introduced in the last chapter. You need to *deeply understand* your consumers' goals, motivations, regulatory approach, and cognitive heuristics.

In the next four chapters, we'll do exactly that. We'll go through each of these four behavioral factors in detail, and I'll end each chapter with questions you can use in your research toward defining and understanding each factor for your consumers.

In Chapter 8, we'll bring all four factors together to determine which of the eighteen mindstates apply to your target consumers. Finally, in Chapter 9, I'll show you how to apply the Mindstate Behavioral Model to your marketing strategy and tactics.

PART TWO

THE MINDSTATE BEHAVIORAL MODEL

To change minds, you must first change the state of mind.

—ROBERT CIALDINI

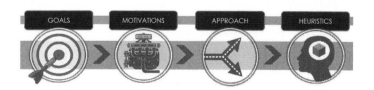

CHAPTER 4

ACTIVATE
THE GOAL

I've been athletic my entire life. I played every sport as a kid. I played high school baseball, and I went into the military, where physical training is a big part of life.

Then, like most people, I settled into life, focused on my career, got married, had a kid, and let myself go. By 2005, I had a beer belly and aching joints, and I couldn't stand the sight of myself. I got more than twenty pounds overweight. I knew I had to make a change. Around the same time, I discovered a triathlon sponsored by the Tom Landry Fitness Center in Dallas. Frankly, I didn't really know what a triathlon even was.

I knew only one thing: I had a goal to lose weight, and training for a triathlon seemed like a great way to reach that goal.

But it was so much deeper than that. I needed to lose weight because I'd lost confidence in myself, and I needed to work toward something that I could succeed in. So I trained. I trained so hard my ass literally came off—all eighteen pounds of it. (OK, I didn't have eighteen pounds of just butt weight, but that sounds better, doesn't it?)

I committed to my goal for nine weeks, which brought me to the night before my first triathlon race in Galveston, Texas. Now, I don't know if you've ever done a race with biking of any kind, but novices like me do whatever stupid trick we can devise to make ourselves faster, even by cutting down your weight on the bike. The only thing I could think to do was get rid of my tire patch, which was meant to save my butt (whatever was left of it) if I ever popped a tire.

It was about the dumbest move I could've made. I saved maybe six ounces getting rid of that tire patch kit. And I can tell you right now that it was not worth it.

I'll give myself credit. I reached mile marker five before my tire popped along the spillway. Now, in a triathlon, you can't ask for help—you have to complete the race yourself—and I had my goal of completing this triathlon if it killed me. I had already lost the weight, and I had already gained back some of my lost confidence, but I hadn't completed this race. It was a symbol of everything I'd worked for, and if I didn't cross the finish line on my own, this whole thing was a failure in my eyes.

I had to finish this race.

So what did I do with the bike on a busted tire? I slung it over my shoulder and ran it the rest of the distance of the triathlon. I expected to take about ninety minutes on the whole race, but in the end, it took me about three and a half hours. In hour two, my wife knew something was wrong and sent my brother-in-law to find me along the route. (Thanks, babe!) He found me limping along the last stage of the race and walked with me until I crossed that damn finish line—one of the very last people to finish that day.

But I finished it. It wasn't enough to want to get in shape—I already had that; I had a higher goal that prompted me to put my bike on my back. I wanted to regain my confidence in myself. I wanted to be a triathlete and feel respected. I wanted to be a winner. That was my emotional, higher-order goal.

Functional goals, like getting into shape, will motivate people only so much. If you can tap into their deeper emotionally driven goals with your messaging, you can get somebody to do something they might not have ever done otherwise, such as carrying a bike on their back to finish a race or buying your product for the first time.

STEP ONE: IDENTIFY AND UNDERSTAND YOUR CONSUMERS' GOALS

The first step in the Mindstate Behavioral Model is to identify, understand, and activate your consumers' goals.

Why? Because goals direct all *actions* and *behaviors*. Without goals, we lack the direction to act on them.

So what do I mean by "goals," exactly? Psychologically, a goal reveals the discrepancy between where we are *now* and where we *want* to be. Or, simply, what we desire in trigger-point moments. It's not any more complicated than that. I like to think of goals as our desired end state. They provide our subconscious with a basic "destination" on which we can focus our attention in the moment and assist us in decision-making behaviors moving forward.

Functionally, goals guide almost all of our behaviors, whether we realize it or not. Goals provide a target for our decisions and actions to move toward and direction for our daily lives. When we act, it's always to move closer to a goal.

And I *do* mean always. Our actions are *always* in response to a goal of some kind. The famous Austrian psychologist Alfred Adler once wrote, "We cannot think, feel, or act without the perception of some goal."

If you're hungry, your goal might be to get a bite to eat. If you're driving, your goal might be to find a nearby parking spot. Or maybe you're at home with a goal of discovering a new recipe on Pinterest.

We have many, many goals that we seek to reach throughout the day, and they direct our focus, attention and actions. But that's a good thing, because without goals, we wouldn't be able to focus, and we'd be lost in our ability to make decisions. Without goals, people simply can't progress in their day or life.

SEEKING OUT HIGHER-ORDER GOALS

Goals provide a desired outcome to reach. They connect consumers' wants to their actions and purchasing behavior.

Goals differ. Goals occur on a spectrum between *functional* and *higher order*.

Functional goals are typically more conscious goals such as the ones on our shopping list or to-do list. We don't tend to assign much emotion to them. *Higher-order* goals are much more aspirational and emotional, so they tap more directly into the key desires of our hearts. These provide an elevated purpose or emotional end state and create stronger reasons to act in our lives.

As a marketer, you should always strive to target and serve people's aspirational, *higher-order* goals. This will create stronger emotional connections between your product and the consumer.

Goals compete for attention. Goals are constantly competing against each other for focus and attention, and certain goals rise to the top. In life, emotional goals almost always take precedence over functional goals. We find passion when we find higher-order goals.

A person might sit at his desk thinking, *OK, my goal right now is to focus on my work.* But five minutes later, a Facebook notification pops up, and the goal shifts. Now he wants to find out what's happening on Facebook. Goals are constantly shifting.

HOW DO CONSUMERS CHOOSE A GOAL TO ACT ON?

Consumers act on goals based on the perceived *suitability*

of that goal in their *current* situational context. Any given situation will make some goals more important than others, and the goal perceived to be most *suitable* in the moment of decision-making will be the winner. Net: the more aspirational (or higher-order) the goal, the more important it is in the moment and the more likely someone acts on that goal.

So as a marketer, ask yourself: What are the common, higher-order consumer goals associated with my brand or category? How can we make these goals top-of-mind in consumers?

To act on a goal, consumers don't have to be conscious of that goal. In fact, consumers aren't consciously aware of their goals *most of the time* they're taking action. They're just pushing toward their goal through subconscious decisions and purchase behaviors.

This is why, as a marketer, your message should focus on marketing to the *subconscious*. And how do you do that?

Goal activation.

Goal activation is simply the act of bringing their key goals to mind. It isn't any more difficult than that. This can be done by simply reminding people of their higher-order, aspirational goals and why those goals are important. Simply show their aspirations back to them.

And remember, every action taken is an attempt to reach a *goal*. Every purchase decision is an action toward a *goal*. Goals matter in marketing.

TO CONNECT, GOALS MUST BE UNDERSTOOD

As a marketer, if you don't know a consumer's goals—especially the higher-order, aspirational goals—you can't empathize with their heart's desires.

If you can't identify and understand your consumer's goals and desires, it's unlikely you'll connect with them *emotionally*. Your stories will sound hollow, and you won't engage with them.

But when you connect with their aspirations, you can evoke a *lot* of emotion in people.

For example, in my company's research for a global brand in the home storage industry, we were hired to talk with people and learn how and why they organize things in different areas of their homes. We learned that people organize things most often to get rid of clutter, so we then looked at what they used as storage devices and why organization was important at a deep, human level.

As we asked these questions in their homes, people gave us a very predictable functional narrative, something like,

"Well, I'm looking for units that are easy to store, fit under my bed, and look good." These were just their basic *functional* goals, however, so we started digging deeper into their aspirational, *higher-order* goals. We found that storage and clutter in the home was a lot more emotionally charged than we ever imagined.

One woman in particular hammered this point home for me.

I stood with this woman in her closet, surveying the space around us. It was an absolute wreck, with clutter everywhere and the faint smell of sweat wafting up my nostrils from the dirty clothes strewn around us.

At first, I asked her about the storage units she could use in the closet to help tidy it up. She responded on the surface level, telling me about the space she could free up and the clutter she could clear.

She spoke to me matter-of-factly. She was a bit embarrassed about her closet clutter, but she was still talking about her functional goal of freeing up closet space. I wanted her to go a layer deeper.

"How does your cluttered closet make you *feel*? Describe the person who has this type of clutter to your best friend. How would they feel deep down?"

Her eyes welled with tears as she looked at the mess around us. She shook her head, almost like she couldn't believe how it had gotten to this point.

"You know," she said, "being in here, looking at this mess—I feel so *embarrassed*. What does it say about me as a *mom*? My job is to take care of my family, but look at this." She gestured to the cluttered closet. "This is absolutely embarrassing."

When she said, "What does it say about me as a *mom?*" I knew exactly what she was feeling. It was pure shame. In her mind, the cluttered closet meant she shouldn't respect herself as a mom and a wife if she couldn't take care of something as small as a closet.

"I can't believe I'm crying about this," she said, shaming herself further.

By showing us her life beyond the *functional* aspects of storage, she showed us the larger, more emotional, *higher-order* problem—shame.

That's what we were looking for. When somebody cries in a closet about a problem your brand can solve, you know you've tapped into something pretty big.

When we tapped into that moment of shame; we knew

better than to limit ourselves to saying, "Our job is to help you organize things." That would have been only a *functional* goal.

Now I knew that our job was to help consumers have less *shame* in their lives. That was a very different place to market from. And we got there by understanding and tapping into that emotional higher-order goal of avoiding shame.

I remember telling the branding team, "From here, your job is *not* to worry about home storage. If you want to look yourself in the mirror in the morning and know why you go to work, here's your mission: you want to stop women from feeling shame in their own home. That's what should keep you up at night.

"We want to lessen *shame*. That's our mantra now," I said. The entire team could relate to this goal and mission. We could all empathize with this emotional goal, and we never would have found it if we hadn't focused on researching both the functional goals and the higher-order goals.

HOW DOES THIS INFLUENCE MARKETING?

As a marketer, your goal is to show how your brand can help people reach their goals. And as you just learned, it's most important to show consumers how your brand meets their aspirations and higher-order goals.

Easy enough. But how do you actually *do* that?

MARKETING TO CONSCIOUS GOALS

You should look at moments in your customers' lives when they are pursuing their goals in your area of influence and determine if they happen to be making decisions *consciously*. Although many decisions are made subconsciously, some are not. When people are close to a deadline, they're often *consciously* trying to reach their goal.

There's no doubt that people do go after goals consciously, and marketers can meet them there.[6] In that type of moment, a functional marketing message could work well: "Our product will help you meet your work deadlines."

MARKETING TO SUBCONSCIOUS GOALS

You can also use the environment and your marketing to activate the deeper, aspirational goal.[7] Perhaps you're a

---

6   Oettingen, Stphens, Mayer, Brinkmann, "Mental Contrasting and the Self-Regulation of Helping Relations," *Social Cognition*, 2010.

7   Moskowitz and Grant, *The Psychology of Goals* (New York: The Guilford Press, 2009).

shoe brand, and you know your consumers typically go to a sporting goods store to buy things other than shoes. But as one man passes the running shoe aisle, he sees your brand's messaging—a photo of a marathoner in your brand's shoes.

He isn't consciously pursuing a goal of buying shoes. But *subconsciously*, he's reminded of another goal of his—get in better shape and run a marathon, all in an effort to earn the badge of respect that comes with completing a marathon. The subconscious activation then *shifts* the goal and makes buying running shoes much more important to him in that moment. Suddenly, he's shopping for shoes, water bottles, and blister-resistant socks, but more importantly, he's buying the immediate *feeling* of accomplishment and doesn't even know why.

Of course, he also could've been at the store for a *conscious* reason. Maybe he knew he wanted to buy shoes. Either way, we as marketers can have some level of control over *both* the conscious and subconscious decision-making of shoppers.

ACTIVATION THROUGH GOALS

The running shoe scenario is a great example of how you can activate *any* goal of interest through a simple activation. When a specific goal is activated, that goal becomes a primary interest for the consumer. Why does that matter? Because now, any communication relating to that goal will be more noticeable, *salient,* and effective.

In the massive amount of messaging clutter in a retail store—with thousands of messages inundating people at any given moment—shoppers will now pick up on their goal more easily. Your display and messaging will be more meaningful, even *subconsciously.* It will literally break through the clutter.

But to achieve this for your brand, you need to clearly identify consumers' goals as they relate to your category.

IDENTIFYING GOALS IN MARKETING RESEARCH

The best way to uncover consumers' functional and higher-order goals is to place the consumers into their actual, *real* context of decision-making.

You don't want to do research in group settings with strangers, such as a traditional focus group. A hotel conference room is not where your consumers make purchase decisions. Putting them in a foreign environment takes away all the context that is *key* to activating their most important functional and higher-order goals in the moment of decision-making. People don't feel shame and cry about clutter in a focus group room.

Instead, research people in the same place they make decisions and interact with your products.

Researching breakfast? Great. Do it in people's *homes*. And do it during *breakfast*. Allow them to actually be in that moment and take on their typical behaviors. All the context and actions happening inside the home are more obvious and notable there.

When doing this research, remove yourself from the environment to the degree you can. Tell the consumer, "Go and make breakfast the way you normally do. Don't notice us or talk with us until breakfast is over, and we'll talk about it together afterward."

Why is this so important? Because when they're in their normal environment, taking on their normal behaviors, they're exposing you to all the contextual factors influencing their psychology and actual behaviors. In these moments of simply observing behaviors, you'll want to look for these types of behaviors:

1. **Nonconsumption.** As you observe people eating breakfast, what are they *not* eating that is available in their home?
2. **Behaviors you would expect to see but don't.** Why aren't they taking on the behaviors you expected?
3. **Workarounds.** Are people working around one prod-

uct to find solutions? Are they adding things to your product to use it? For example, if people commonly add honey to your cereal or mix it with other cereal, that's a valuable insight.

4. **Task avoidance.** While people are interacting with your product, you may find they choose not to use one element of it. Maybe you notice that every time someone opens a box of cereal. They're taking out the bag and putting it in a plastic container. They're avoiding the box. That's an issue. You need to look for those things.

RESEARCH INTERVIEW BEST PRACTICES

- Sitting face-to-face across a table with someone to interview them never works as well as being active in the moment with them. When you interact with people in everyday situations, such as going for a walk, you break down the interviewer-interviewee relationship and provide a sense of ease and comfort that helps them open up.

- Likewise, talking to people in their homes or workplaces makes them much more comfortable than talking in a controlled environment such as a research facility or conference room. Sterile, uncomfortable environments give you sterile, uncomfortable conversations.

- Asking someone for his feedback on a product or experience immediately after use or consumption often yields inflated feedback. Wait a few days before seeking feedback. Although their memories may be a bit less accurate, their passion for your product or service will be spot-on.

- Be open with who you are and what you need. Researchers often hide their intentions from respondents, which can create tension. You don't have to go into excruciating detail, but letting people know the basics of the study and what you want often creates a partnership between you and your consumer.

FUNCTIONAL VERSUS HIGHER ORDER

As you would expect, it's easier to get people to discuss functional goals than the aspirational, higher-order ones that can make them a bit nervous when discussing.

Identifying the functional goals can be as simple as asking people, "What are you trying to accomplish in this moment?" People will often respond with a list, full of things such as, "I'm trying to finish the meal quickly," or, "I'm trying to make sure it doesn't make a mess."

But when it comes to researching a consumer's higher-order, aspirational goals, it's tough to trust their answers. Why? Because people can't often reliably access these without some great effort. Many times they don't truly know *why* they do what they do.

Most people would be embarrassed to admit they don't know why they do what they do, so they come up with post-rationalized benefits and reasons for their actions. And this is *exactly* why you need to get people outside of that rational space if you want to find their higher-order goals.

ONE IMPORTANT QUESTION

To find the more aspirational, higher-order goals of a consumer, ask this question: "Beyond the functional benefit of this product or service, what's the benefit to your *life*? How is this going to make your *life* better?"

Start with the category you're in. Let's say it's cereal. If you ask, "What are you looking for in a cereal?" you'll get the typical responses: "Great taste. Low price. Somewhat healthy."

That type of response isn't going to help you differentiate your brand from any competition. You can just lower the price or add sweetener. Fine. So can everyone else.

But if you ask, "How does cereal benefit you in your *life*?" Now you start getting into the good stuff.

"Well," the mother might reply, "this cereal helps me provide a hearty meal for my child in the morning when I have only twenty minutes with him before he leaves me for the entire day. I use cereal as a way to sit down with him and have a moment with him. And he's going to enjoy eating with me and have a better conversation because he likes the cereal."

"Also," she might continue, "I like to know he's full and energized and ready to learn at school. He's not going to lose focus, and he's not going to have hunger pangs. I'm sending my kid out by himself, but that's one thing I don't have to worry about. It makes me feel like a good mom."

See the difference? That's a *totally* different space and opportunity for your brand to become a part of. Now I can innovate around those goals and ask, "How can we create more of these important moments?"

Your marketing doesn't have to always be about the cereal itself or its functional benefits. It can be about these higher-order goals and aspirational, heroic moments people want.

SEVEN MORE STRATEGIES TO USE

Here are seven additional strategies you can use to uncover subconscious, highly emotional goals:

1. **Projective-based techniques.** In psychology, we use this term to mean "projecting outside oneself." People who are not thinking about themselves are more able to tap into subconscious, higher-order emotional drivers of behavior. Techniques include laddering, which means you keep asking why until you get to the higher-order goals. Projective techniques help you ladder from functional goals to higher-order ones.
2. **Storytelling.** When people tell stories, they often reveal the important things that are subconsciously influencing them. Rather than asking people, "Tell me why it's so important for you to put this cereal into a box," you can say, "Why don't you give me a

story? Tell me about the very first time you ate Honey Nut Cheerios."

3. **Image sorting.** Ask people to sort through different images and talk through why they put images into one category versus another. You can assign the categories or just say, "Put these images into different categories that make sense to you."

4. **Collage building.** Using only a few pictures, ask people to use the images to build a narrative or story that explains how and why they use your products.

5. **Third-party role-playing.** We ask people to pretend to be some other being. We might say, "Imagine you're an alien and you just flew to Earth and landed on top of your house. I want you to report back to your alien civilization what you're seeing and what doesn't make any sense to you." People will see things in their behaviors that they wouldn't have seen otherwise.

6. **Personification.** This is where we say, "Hey, if this brand were a superhero, what would be its traits? What type of superhero would it be? Why?" We might hear things such as, "Well, if this brand were a superhero, it'd be Superman." Why? "Well, Superman is fast and indestructible," they might say. And if they did, you'd be getting the clear message that people associate the brand with speed and strength.

7. **Deprivation.** We ask, "What would you do if you didn't have this brand of cereal? What would you eat? Would you choose not to eat cereal at all? Would you

choose not to eat *breakfast* at all?" Deprivation helps you understand the broader context of how cereal, in this case, fits into people's broader lives. You might hear things such as, "I'll have waffles. Or maybe I'd just grab a piece of cake."

BONUS: NINE MORE WAYS TO IDENTIFY GOALS

In addition to the strategies we've discussed, how else can you understand people's functional and aspirational, higher-order goals?

Here is one high-level question and nine specific follow-up questions to use in your research conversations with consumers.

First, the broader question to get them started:

"Tell me the story of the last purchase you made or the last time you used this category. Visualize it. I want you to be very specific. Tell me the story of why you desired the product. Walk me through the entire story, from desiring it, to buying it, to using it. What was the result?"

From there, you want to understand the consumers' life objectives and how the product fits (or doesn't fit) within those goals. Here are the nine follow-up questions I find most helpful:

1. When did you first start thinking about the need for this product? Go back to that time. Tell me what the situation was and why you needed it.

2. Was anyone else involved? Were other people's interests or preference involved in that final decision?

3. What would have been the ideal solution that day?

4. How did the product make you feel when you bought it and used it? What feelings are most important to you in that situation?

5. How does the product fit into the broader goals you're trying to accomplish today?

6. What would you do if this product were not available? Would you go to another brand? Would you choose not to buy the product at all? Would you go to a totally different category?

7. If you would choose a different solution, how would you decide between what you bought and any other option? What helps you decide on this versus another brand?

8. What were you using before you found this product? How is this specifically better?

9. How do you currently use it? Show me, if you can, but be specific. (Get them to use your product, website, or whatever, and just observe. Identify the steps of how they use it.)

You'll take this information and summarize the goals people have as they relate to your brand or product. In the end, you'll be able to answer the question: What's their ideal situation, given their deeper goals?

And with that, the first step of the Mindstate Behavioral Model will be complete.

NEXT STEPS

You've discovered your consumers' higher-order goals by placing them in the context they consume your product in, then laddered why questions or used projective techniques until you fully understand the emotional and contextual drivers behind their behaviors.

The next step?

Understanding *why* your consumers want what they want.

CHAPTER 5

PRIME THE NEED

A prime is anything in your environment that has strong associations that come to mind once you are exposed to it. Let me give you a very famous example: French music.

Imagine you're walking down the aisle at the grocery store, shopping for dinner. What music is playing? Do you even pay attention to it? If you're like most people, the answer is no. But the truth is, your subconscious mind is being primed to make certain decisions by the music choice in the grocery store.

French music played in the background of a grocery store may bring up subconscious associations linked to France—great food, berets, long cigarettes, and great wine.

Here's why this is important. Let's say you go through the bakery looking for bread. Because the French music primes you to think about all things related to France, you're more likely to notice and actually choose the bread that has packaging with a French flag on it. Why? The associations you have with France are more top-of-mind because of the music, and therefore, your subconscious mind links these positive associations to the bread with the French flag.

Now imagine you move to the produce section and see all of these glistening fruits and vegetables. Suddenly, you hear thunder and lightning. Is it a freak midday storm in the grocery store? No, it's coming from the vegetable section. Many grocery stores spray water on the vegetables and accompany it with the sound of thunder to prime your association of vegetables with nature and freshness.

The water spray doesn't enhance freshness in the least. In fact, it makes the produce rot faster. But guess what? The grocery stores don't care about the waste, because the priming of the water and thunder is so effective in driving vegetable, fruit, and impulse sales throughout the store that it compensates for the lost inventory to rotting.

Amazing, right? Well, you haven't seen anything yet.

This brings us to the second step in the Mindstate Behavioral Model: understanding *why* consumers want what they want. If you can understand that, you'll know how to create a powerful emotional engine that propels them to take action toward reaching their goals.

So where do we begin?

Motivational psychology.

WHAT EXACTLY IS MOTIVATION?

When it comes to the definition of motivation, the consensus seems to be that motivation is an internal state or condition that activates and *energizes* behavior.

If goals provide us with a destination, motivations move us to *action*. Motivation is the emotional fuel that drive us toward our functional and higher-order goals.

Every action a person takes has an underlying motivation behind it. Motivations drive you to watch a movie. They drive your desire to throw a kick-ass birthday party for your son. And they drive you to buy the brands you buy and visit the websites you visit.

Motivations drive people at a deep emotional level. Understanding people's true motivations will help you shift people from *intending to act* into actually *acting*.

Motivations keep people progressing toward their goals despite resistance. Resistance could be something as small as a pop-up ad distracting someone whose goal was to buy something else. Understanding motivations helps you create an incentive for consumers to overcome resistance and act.

When we talk about emotional marketing, what we're really talking about is *motivational* marketing. The emotion in advertising is directly tied to the underlying human motivation.

NEW BREAKTHROUGHS AND INSIGHTS

Motivational psychology has been studied since the mid-eighteenth century, and we have well over a hundred years of science focused on understanding the motivations that drive humans to take action. But until the mid-1990s and the advent of the internet, theories were all over the place.

What happened? The internet made it easier to unify and understand all the motivations. It made it easier to see how people are heavily influenced by varying motivations, depending on their differing situations and contexts.

THE NINE HUMAN MOTIVATIONS

After years of studying motivational psychology for our clients—particularly Reiss's research on universal human needs and self-determination theory[8]—we have identified nine distinct psychological motivations that drive the majority of our decisions and actions.

These nine motivations *drive* people psychologically and incentivize them to pursue their goals. These motivations are universal to *all* people—all demographics, age groups, and cultures.

The nine human motivations also have minimal overlap. It's possible for one motivation to build on another, and it's also possible to see two or three different motivations working together. However, there will always be one primary motivation. Anything else is just a secondary motivation.

An entire book could be written for each of these nine human motivations, and I'm not going to attempt to stuff thirty years of motivational psychology research into this chapter. Instead, what follows is a high-level definition of each of the nine motivations we see in our research and use in the Mindstate Behavioral Model. I'll let you take

---

8   Steven Reiss, "Intrinsic and Extrinsic Motivation," *Teaching of Psychology* 39, no. 2 (2012): 152–156.

it upon yourself to delve more deeply into the specific motivations that make the most sense for your business.

These nine motivations live inside *every* consumer at various points. People can be in a mindstate with any of these motivations, toward any type of goal.

Here are the nine core motivations, in alphabetical order:

ACHIEVEMENT

Achievement is the feeling of being successful, victorious, and proud by overcoming obstacles.

Along with Nike, Bosch Power Tools is a brand in this space. When consumers want to be achievers and desire success, they want tools and resources that help them succeed.

AUTONOMY

Autonomy is the feeling of being unique and independent and having a feeling of self-determination in one's actions.

LEGO is a brand in this space. The blocks let consumers express themselves and create unique experiences and products. *The LEGO Movie* reinforces the idea that the real power of creative expression is to make things that are unique to you. Boutique store brands are also in this space, conveying the ideas of uniqueness and independence.

Consumers who are driven by this motivation will seek freedom and the tools and resources that help them customize a product or experience on their terms.

BELONGING

Belonging is the feeling of being aligned, accepted, and connected with others.

Several brands come to mind in this space. Harley-Davidson evokes this idea of the in-group and special privilege. If you have a Harley, you *belong*. CrossFit and professional sports teams also tap into the motivation of belonging.

Consumers driven by this motivation will seek products and services that help them feel accepted and part of a tribe or connected with others.

COMPETENCE

Competence is the feeling of being *capable* by being qualified, prepared, and skilled in an activity.

Microsoft and Home Depot are competence brands. When consumers go into Home Depot, they're trying to feel competence in a home improvement project. People influenced by the competence motivation are looking for tools and resources to feel more skilled and capable when they need to act.

EMPOWERMENT

Empowerment is the feeling of being authorized and equipped to act on desired choices.

It might seem random, but Doritos and Samsung are examples of empowerment brands. For several of the recent Super Bowls, Doritos empowered their consumers to create their own commercials, the best of which would be featured in the big game. Likewise, Samsung positioned itself as an empowerment brand by showing customers what they could accomplish with its technology. Consumers driven by empowerment want to feel in control and look for the ability to manage the environment around them.

ENGAGEMENT

Engagement is the ongoing feeling of being captivated, excited, and interested in an activity.

When I think of engagement brands, I think of Disney.

I also think of IKEA stores, movies, concerts, and even food brands such as Kellogg's. Consumers buy all of those brands to engage their senses.

The engagement of nostalgia brands plays in this space, too. People may buy old-time cereal brands such as Rice Krispies for the nostalgic memories more than the actual taste of the cereal.

Engagement seekers are looking for brands that engage their senses and provide a feeling of relief and release from the world.

ESTEEM

Esteem is the feeling of being approved, respected, and admired by others.

Consumers buy luxury brands such as Lexus, BMW, and Chanel when influenced by this motivation. In addition to luxury brands, social media sites often appeal to people motivated by esteem. Esteem is often what drives people to post photos online and feel good when other users like it.

Esteem-driven consumers want to feel respected by others and seek tools or resources that make them feel more socially admired.

NURTURANCE

Nurturance is the feeling of being appreciated, loved, and taken care of by others. It's also the feeling of having the ability to take care of others.

Gerber and Hallmark are great nurturance brands. Those brands build connections with consumers by helping them feel loved by others or nurturing to others.

SECURITY

Security is feeling safe and protected from threats.

Home security brands such as ADT and life insurance brands such as New York Life are strong security brands. People who are driven by security seek to feel safe and are looking for products or services that provide protection from physical or emotional harm.

In our research, we find that products and services tend to be associated with one to three of these nine motivations. Whether you know it or not, your brand is, too. Nike certainly knows it's an achievement brand, even if consumers' exact motivation around achievement isn't always known. Nike is also associated with belonging and esteem, as most sports brands are.

As a marketer, you're the best judge of which motivations

your brand should be focusing on. To identify these motivations, ask yourself, "Which motivations best describe how my customers want to *feel* in the moment of buying or using my brand?"

Do they want to feel more successful? Speak to them about how your brand can make them an achiever. That's how to connect with their hearts. It's that simple.

HOW DO THESE MOTIVATION TYPES WORK?

Here are a few examples of how these motivations could work to help create the emotional drive to buy your brand over others. First, let's look at people with a goal of losing ten pounds. For some of these people, the motivator could be esteem—maybe they want to feel more respected at work. For them, if you have a product that can help them lose the weight, you could literally market it as being important for how others see them and their esteem.

Another group of dieters could be driven by the motivation of security. Maybe it's a dad who wants to lose the weight because he's worried about his heart health and he wants to live to see his daughter's wedding. If that's your target consumer, you may want to talk about your brand in terms of providing security: "Our product will help you be there for your family in the future."

Those people all have the same goal of losing ten pounds, but the message should be very different to each of them based on their very different motivations.

Similarly, what might motivate a consumer to buy organic food? Are the buyers driven by belonging? If so, they might say something like, "I want to be part of something bigger than myself." They may want to belong to the group of people who believe in natural products and make purchases based on the impact to the environment.

However, nurturance could also be the primary motivation of an organic food buyer. Maybe they're saying something like, "You know what? I just don't want chemicals in my family's food." They want to show their love for their family by providing them with healthy, non-GMO foods.

As a marketer, when you understand the core motivations in play when consumers make a category decision, you get clear direction on how to prime that need and associate it with your brand. That understanding should also guide your overall messaging and brand strategy.

WHERE DOES MOTIVATION MEET MARKETING?

Understanding motivations will elevate your marketing by reinforcing a consumer's *aspirational* identity—who they want to be. It will position your brand as helping a consumer bridge the gap between where they are today and where they *want* to be.

It's easy to see how motivations will affect how you design your marketing creative and influence your consumers.

Some of the most loved and iconic brands in the world are built around the core human motivations. Brands such as Nike and Harley-Davidson didn't become iconic by making shoes or motorcycles. They got there because they helped consumers see themselves as who they *want* to be. When you tap into the core human motivation, you can help people reach (or at least take action toward) their aspirations and higher-order goals.

Clients often ask me, "What's the one piece of advice you would give me?" I tell them, "You'd better know the underlying motivations for your brand."

And by underlying motivations, again, I'm talking about finding the primary one or two motivations—*not* attempting to serve all nine. If you try to serve all nine motivations and tap into the entire market, you're not going to tap into *anybody*. Your message won't be strong enough or focused enough. Believe me when I tell you this; I see it happen all the time, and it has disastrous results. You'll dilute the equity of your brand and lower the incentive to act.

Most sophisticated marketers want to find their brand's story and their unique selling proposition. The brand story and selling proposition can be solidified by building a framework around the primary human motivations that drive people to choose your brand.

PRIMING A DEEPER CONNECTION

In short, a motivation is something that pushes someone toward their goal. This distinction was made clear to me when a shoe polish company approached TriggerPoint with a problem. Their customers in Indonesia weren't buying their brand of polish as much as they used to. After a lot of failed innovation launches and no significant impact from their brand marketing or pricing strategy, they came to us for help. They wanted to use behavioral science to figure out what was really causing the drop in sales and how they could sell more polish.

In order to solve the shoe polish company's problem, we had to discover people's deep emotional motivations for buying shoe polish. So we packed up the team, flew to Jakarta, and spoke with mothers inside of their homes with their children to discuss shoes. Most of the women I spoke to did not have much money, and their homes were very, very small. As is customary with our projects, we started our conversations about life and their goals for raising their children. What happened next was incredibly surprising to us all.

The moms talked about how important it was for their children to have polished shoes. Why? It would be easy to assume that it was because they didn't have much money and needed their children's shoes to last longer. If that was the case, it could lead to a brand story like, "Our shoe polish will make your shoes last a long time."

In this case, that assumption would've been wrong. When we explored this need through a motivational lens and uncovered what *truly* motivated the moms, we found *nurturance* to be a deeper motivation for them.

Kids get bullied everywhere, and Indonesia is no different. In that country, kids get bullied for many things, including wearing shoes with scuff marks or holes. So moms looked at shoe polish as a small way to show their love for their kids and nurture them. If they couldn't afford new shoes, they could at least cover up their old shoes and make them look new.

It was a beautiful realization because the moms' motivation to provide nurturance to their children was a much deeper, stronger emotional connection to shoe polish than the functional benefit of protecting shoes. It's something that every mom could relate to and was just a small messaging tweak we used to prime this motivation in subsequent ads. This small tweak has since been used to help turn around the business globally.

As a marketer, your job is to *prime* that motivational desire.

In that case, you're going to focus on nurturance. That's going to drive your consumers' higher-order goals for the category and make them choose you over other options available to them. If you don't prime that motivation desire in your marketing, you'll never connect on that deep, emotional level like we did in Indonesia.

So let's say you're a retailer, and you have a goal to differentiate yourself in the marketplace. Your messaging says, "You'll save more money at my store." That's a great functional goal, and if you talk about saving money, you can make people feel better about shopping. That's good, and you can certainly use that in your marketing.

But if you understand a consumer's *higher-order* goal and map your motivation to their aspirations, it changes everything. A higher-order goal might be, "I want to save money so I can take my son to Disney World." And *that's* about nurturance. That makes them feel like a hero.

Now you can trigger a deeper emotional connection with your store or website. You can send a subtle message: "By shopping with us, you'll be a better, more nurturing, loving parent to your child."

The higher-order goals are where you build the strongest desire to use your product or service. That's why you want your brand to be associated with the key motivation that drives consumer decisions in your category.

HOW DO YOU IDENTIFY CORE MOTIVATIONS?

There are several tactics that can be used to identify which of our nine core human motivations drive your consumers to action. Again, the most important thing is to research consumers in the actual place where they make their category decisions.

If that's in bed at night, that's where you should be talking to them. If they make decisions on a particular website, you should have them using that website. If it's in a shopping aisle, you should talk with them there.

From there, use any or all of the following proven tactics to find and understand your consumers' deepest and strongest motivations.

STRESS RESPONSE

Increase stress response by distracting them or placing them under time limits. When people are under *slight* stress, they're more likely to tap into their subconscious System 1 thinking, while also allowing for System 2 thinking and justification.

As we talked about before, consumers often make decisions using both System 1 and System 2. There's a balance of both of those, so you want to initiate System 1 thinking by putting people under stress but not under so much stress that they have to "turn off" System 2 and make an immediate decision. You want both.

When they're rushed by time constraints or other slight pressure, they don't have time to take into account all the factors that are in play. Instead, they're going to rely on psychological shortcuts and System 1 processing. This will help to reveal their deeper motivations.

IMAGE SORTING

We often place people under a time constraint and show them forty to sixty images that represent each of our nine core motivations. Then I'll tell them to categorize the images based on their own interpretations. For example, I might tell them to categorize all the images into piles that make them similar, or how you'd like to feel after using a particular brand.

When the images are all sorted into piles, talk to them about the piles they made and why they were organized in this fashion. You'll ask, "What made you group these images together?"

With one particular pile, they may say something like, "Well, these are about being a good dad." Maybe there's an image of a dad holding hands with his kid. Maybe another picture shows a smiling child.

"Tell me what's going on in these pictures," you might say.

"Well, gosh," they might reply, "this is what I want my child to feel."

"Well, why is that?" you ask. "Why would that be important to you?"

"Well, if my child is happy," they reply, "I know that I've given them love."

Boom! Nurturance. Through image sorting, you've just figured out that nurturance is at least one of the core motivations for this guy.

MORE IMAGE EXERCISES

Additionally, you can simply show people pictures that map back to the nine core motivations and ask them to name the first thing that comes to mind and if it's a desired feeling or not. Once again, place people under stress by moving quickly through the pictures or create distractions. Their initial reaction is the key to understanding their core motivation. Ask them to go with their gut. Don't overthink this.

When people look at images, they access areas of their brain they otherwise wouldn't know. You often hear things such as, "I never knew I felt like this." It's not because they were too embarrassed to give their opinion. It's because they truly didn't *know* their feelings until they talked about each picture.

The classic example I've seen often is when people focus on images of shields, walls, or badges. When I point out, "Seems like in a lot of your pictures, walls are a common theme," they might say, "You know, I've noticed that, too."

So I'll ask, "Why do you think that is?"

They may say, "I've never thought about it, but maybe I'm feeling a little bit restless and kind of scared. I guess I might be fearful that I need protection."

Bam! Security motivation.

And they wouldn't have picked that up unless they noticed the commonality of all these pictures. The images allow people to access their subconscious in a way they'd never be able to if you just asked them to think harder about what their primary motivations are. "Think harder" are System 2 words. With those directions, people will stop at, "I just want to save money."

You want people to access their System 1. Ask them to *feel*.

To round out our list of research tactics, marketers should consider using two creative exercises: drawing and role-playing.

In a projected drawing exercise (or any type of fill-in-the-blank exercise), you'd ask this type of question: "Draw for me a situation where you would be a great dad." If they say that being a great father means showing affection, loving their child, and protecting their family, you know they're motivated by nurturance and security.

For creative role-playing, place people into situations of authority and power. "I want you to pretend you are the CEO of Walmart," you could say. "I want you, as a person in a position of authority, to tell us the ideal experience for someone who buys this product. What would make a five-star experience? How about a six-star? Seven?" The more you let people talk and play out the role, the more likely they'll speak about what drives the ideal experience, and you'll recognize their underlying motivations.

NEXT STEPS

It's important to understand the nine core human

motivations that drive people to go after their goals. By understanding each of those motivations, you can create messaging that creates an emotional purpose to act, which is the necessary engine to drive people to your brand.

Your next step is understanding the different *approaches* your consumers take when they act toward their goals.

CHAPTER 6

FRAME THE CHOICE

The next part of our model requires understanding how people "approach" their goals. This is a psychological concept called regulatory focus. Think of it as our internal GPS or Waze app that tells us the path we should take to reach our goals. And once you have insight into the regulatory focus of your target consumers, you can *frame* your brand's benefits with visuals and copy that provide a path of least resistance for their subconscious to follow. This in itself will lower psychological resistance and friction in your marketing creative. By doing so, you can make it psychologically natural and easy for them to choose your brand.

See, in today's over-saturated world of marketing, people have become more and more resistant to all forms of marketing. Framing is the psychological means to lower resistance to marketing and decisions so that they feel more intuitive and natural.

Framing works on any goals you have, in business and in life. You don't even have to sell anything to utilize framing. Just look at my son, Nicholas, and how I use framing to overcome his aversion to vegetables. Mindstates in parenting!

FRAMING VEGETABLES TO NICHOLAS

Nicholas *hates* vegetables.

He has always hated vegetables. Like any other red-blooded American boy, he loves pizza and McDonald's (although I think that the Happy Meal toy plays a big part in that love). And if your kid is like mine, you too know that it's almost impossible to get them to eat vegetables at dinner on a consistent basis. So I'm going to give you, my reader, a scientifically proven way to use psychology—specifically, regulatory focus—to get your kid to eat them.

I'm a behavioral scientist, so I study Nicholas very closely. He's quite fascinating from a behavioral psychology perspective. And one thing I know for sure is that Nicholas is naturally much more optimistic or promotion-focused, particularly as it relates to food. He's always thinking of the upside or good things that will happen when he eats. In fact, he sees dinner as a way to get what he really wants: a sweet dessert and some extra TV time before bed. Dinner and food provide him more *good,* in his eyes, and he focuses on all the great things that dinner can give him. That's just who he is.

I am more cautious or prevention-focused (risk-averse) in general, so I generally approach food through a different lens. I'm generally more concerned with the consequences *or bad* things that might happen if I eat the wrong food, particularly those chicken wings from the sports bar down the street.

Because Nicholas is more optimistic-focused, I frame eating vegetables in a way that creates the path of least resistance for him. If I want Nicholas to eat more veggies, I need to help him focus on what he can *gain* from eating them. So the first thing we instituted in our home when he was a young kid was the rule of the happy plate. A "happy plate" is one with all the veggies eaten off it. So almost daily, I remind him, "You can only get dessert if you make a happy plate!" With this new frame, he looks at his plate as the pathway to dessert and does what he can to stomach a few bites of broccoli.

Then he'll ask, "Daddy, Daddy, is it a happy plate?" And I say, "Not yet." We go through this back-and-forth dance until we feel that he has gotten about as much greens into him as possible, and we let him get a dessert.

He'll continue to eat the vegetables, but not because he wants to eat them. He does it because he's optimistically focusing on *gaining the reward* he'll get from having a "happy plate."

But sometimes the "happy plate" strategy doesn't work. In that case, I'll employ a second strategy.

Nicholas *loves* Marvel superheroes. He actually wants to *be* a superhero. So the second strategy is to associate the veggies with what (or who) he wants to be. "Nick," I tell him, "if you eat your vegetables, you'll be *more* like *Spiderman*. You can do *flips*."

Last, visualization of the goal is another strategy that can be used for Nick's optimistic focus to eating. Before dinner, I'll sometimes call him over to the freezer, open the door, and ask him to pick out the exact cup of ice cream he wants. I let him hold that ice cream and look at it.

Then I make him put it back and close the freezer door himself.

Horrible, right?

But here's the thing: if he can visualize that ice cream and he can focus on *gaining* it as a reward, I'm *much* more likely to get him to eat vegetables.

Some strategies I tried haven't worked. Why? Because they were either cautious or prevention-focused strategies. For example:

- "Nick, you can't leave the table until you eat your veggies." In his world, that's great, because if he doesn't leave the table, he can't take a bath. If he really holds out, he might not have to go to sleep or to school. He's thinking, *I'll play that game.* He's OK with that.
- "Nick, if you don't eat your veggies, you'll get sick." But getting sick is another reason he wouldn't have to go to school.

- "You'll lose your teeth." That didn't work either, because, thanks to the Tooth Fairy, teeth are his source of income. So he's like, "Yeah!"

Sure, I might eventually get him to eat vegetables with these prevention-focused, cautious strategies and make him and myself miserable in the process. But why would I do that when I *know* that an optimistic-focused strategy is the path of least resistance for him? Knowing that makes both of our lives much easier.

Similarly, brands that know the dominant regulatory approach of their target consumers can also create a path of least resistance and help influence their behaviors.

Once you understand the underlying motivations that drive your consumers to pursue their goals, the next step is to understand the psychological strategy they most often take to *approach* and pursue their goals, and map your creative to fit it. This is a concept called regulatory fit.

WHAT IS THE REGULATORY FIT THEORY?

Regulatory fit theory is a *goal-pursuit* theory, placing special emphasis on the relation between the motivational orientation of the person making the decision and the manner in which that person pursues the goal.

The idea was pioneered by E. Tory Higgins, who wrote a book with Heidi Grant Halvorson called *Focus: Use Different Ways of Seeing the World for Success and Influence.* In it, they wrote the following:

> How you experience the world around you, what you pay attention to, how you interpret it, and how much you care about it will be determined, to a large degree, by your motivational focus at the moment.

According to Higgins's research, people pursue their goals using one of two approaches: a *promotion* (i.e. optimistic) approach or a *prevention* (i.e. cautious) approach.

So what are the differences between the two?

OPTIMISTIC APPROACH

People with this approach seek strategies that help them maximize their chances of successfully reaching their goal.

For example, a person with a goal to lose weight who uses an optimistic approach might adopt a strategy of eating more healthfully. If you're a marketer and you position your weight-loss product as a way to help that person eat better, the product will feel more in line with that person's weight-loss strategy. For example, if my product is a health food snack like Wicked Crisps and I know they pursue this goal using an optimistic approach, I'll focus on talking about the extra vitamins and nutrients you'll get by eating my snack. In other words, my messaging will key in on what you can *gain* by eating the snack.

That message will be psychologically framed in a way that will feel *natural* to the consumer who's optimistic in nature because it's helping him *maximize* his chance of success.

CAUTIOUS APPROACH

Now look at the same goal and the same motivation, but this time the person is driven by a prevention regulatory focus—or is more cautious in their approach to eating healthy. That means they're seeking strategies to *minimize* their chances of loss. They're more focused on "avoiding the chance of eating poorly."

Instead of seeking to eat more healthful food, their strategy is to stay away from junk or fast-food, maybe desserts. Under these conditions, you'd want to frame up your brand as a way of helping her *avoid negative consequences*. For example, if I know that same health food snack has consumers who are more cautious in their approach to food, I'll craft the messaging to underscore the fact that it has *no trans fats and fewer calories* than the alternative.

In short, the messaging will focus on the unhealthy consequences or risks they will *prevent* by eating healthy.

If your product speaks to her that way, it's going to feel much more natural.

Same goal, same motivation. Different strategy in how you frame your product to your customer.

WHICH APPROACH IS BEST?

Neither. There is no good or bad regulatory focus. They're just strategies (often subconscious) people use to reach their goals. Most of us use both approaches throughout the day but for different purposes in different situations.

Look at a millennial woman who is a new mom and is in the workforce. At work, she may be driven by the achievement motivation. She may seek opportunities and try to maximize her chance of advancement. She uses an optimistic approach to her career.

But as a first-time mom, she may also use a *cautious approach* for decisions related to her new baby. She's scared of doing something wrong, and she'll make decisions that help her minimize her chances of risk to her new baby.

So how can you tell which regulatory focus or approach is being used by your customer?

Listen closely to how they talk about your brand to others. When they tell others about *why* they use your brand, they will frame it as a way to gain benefits or a way to avoid negatives.

GREENPEACE AND CAUTIOUS FOCUS

Some time ago, I worked on a project with Greenpeace International. In their fundraising and messaging, they were primarily using a cautious messaging strategy to drive donor engagement. Donations and volunteering would help prevent bad consequences for the environment and the planet. That's why you typically saw pictures of polar bears stranded on broken-up ice caps or the ugly effects of pollution. It's a classic communications strategy with almost all nonprofits, and it's dead wrong.

We did a behavioral study that found it was *much* more effective to talk to potential donors in an optimistic-focused way. We found that people—especially the older and higher-income people who spend time and money on environmental causes—were less focused on trying to prevent bad outcomes and more focused on how their support would make the world *better.*

With this information in hand, Greenpeace began to talk about the upsides of saving the planet versus the downsides of not saving it. For example, we showed that when Germany moved from coal to solar power, it created thousands more jobs.

That new approach resulted in a *dramatic* increase of social media engagement for Greenpeace.

I'm not saying that a cautious, prevention-focused strategy never worked for Greenpeace, but optimism simply works consistently better on their older, higher-income donors.

Both approaches—optimistic and cautious—can have success. As a marketer, your job is to find the approach that fits best with the target consumers' natural inclinations and frame your brand to match their subconscious instinct.

HOW THIS WORKS (AND HOW IT DOESN'T)

Regulatory fit theory *massively* impacts your marketing strategy and tactics. Why? Because it can help you psychologically frame your brand in a way that aligns with the way people *subconsciously* approach decision-making in the category.

When aligned well, this framing effect makes your marketing more salient, fluid, and intuitive to your customers. It creates a marketing copy road map to drive behavior change, not only because it feels natural, but also because the brand feels more *relatable*. Consumers will feel that the brand "gets" them and will lower their resistance to your offer.

When your brand story aligns this well with consumers and feels natural and relatable, the messaging then becomes more *believable*. These consumers won't need more evidence or justification because they've got a deeper emotional connection with your brand.

THE CONSEQUENCES OF TRADITIONAL RESEARCH IN THIS AREA

If your marketing and messaging is off and not aligned well with consumers' regulatory focus, they're going to be less engaged. Your brand is going to be less trustworthy and less relatable.

When you try to figure out why consumers didn't choose your brand, traditional research won't help you much. It's as simple as that.

In a traditional focus group, participants are *not* going to say, "Oh, you know, your messaging is focused on using an optimistic approach, but I'm much more cautious-focused." Consumers don't often know that about themselves.

Instead, they'll say things such as, "This product seems *OK*, I guess." They'll hesitate. They'll pause because their true feelings are beyond their consciousness. But consciously, they'll try to come up with some type of explanation.

They might say, "I kind of like how this looks, and I agree with this message." But that's a passive statement. Something's lacking.

When I'm in a situation like that, as a marketer, I don't sit there and think, *OK, well, I guess we just need to be more emotionally engaging.* Instead, my first thought is this: *Did we write the copy using a cautious frame? Maybe that's where we're off.*

Whether it's in a focus group or in an actual shopping environment, consumers are unlikely to consciously reject your message outright. They're unlikely to say, "I disagree with your message." It's much more likely they'll simply *delay* their decision. They'll just say or think, consciously or subconsciously, "Something's a little off. I'll come back to that later."

And that's the kiss of death in today's world. They'll never be back.

HOW DO I APPLY THIS TO MY MARKETING?

Here are some basic strategies to use when applying regulatory fit theory to your marketing and messaging. These are specific tactics to make your product or service feel natural and relatable to somebody in an optimistic state of mind or a *cautious* state of mind.

> Again, in an attempt to be a practical guide, I'm not going to go into the many deep nuances of regulatory focus. For a more thorough understanding of this theory, I'd encourage you to read the book *Focus: Use Different Ways of Seeing the World for Success and Influence* by Heidi Grant Halvorson and E. Tory Higgins.

STRATEGIES FOR OPTIMISTIC (VERSUS CAUTIOUS)

To frame your brand's benefits in a way that matches people's regulatory focus, here are some general guidelines to help your creative tap into consumers' optimistic/*promotion* regulatory focus (versus the *cautious/prevention* focus, which follows in parentheses):

- Focus on pleasure (versus pain).
- Highlight the benefits of success (versus the cost of failure).
- Talk about the desire for growth (versus the desire for security or the possibility of rejection).
- Emphasize why your product makes sense and why it works. Say things such as, "We have the very best scientists focused on making sure our product is the

best," (versus emphasizing the scientific facts that prove the product is the best).

- Accentuate feelings (versus facts and reasons).
- Show emotions that are cheerful (versus relaxing).
- Be more independent, say "you" (instead of "them"). Optimistic-focused people want a feeling of independence, so address the individual rather than the group. (People in cautious mode find comfort in the interdependence of people.)
- Emphasize taking chances, making changes, and seizing opportunities (versus stability).
- Emphasize speed, progress, and the whole product (versus accuracy, control, or stability of all of a system's individual parts).
- Use animated gestures (versus reserved gestures).
- Use faster speeds and cadences in speaking, videos, and songs (versus slower).

These are just a few beginner strategies to use for a better fit with your customers' natural regulatory state. With these in hand, you can generate literally thousands of visual and copy combinations to scientifically frame your creative in a way that increases emotional engagement and lowers friction to your ideas.

But it goes even deeper than that.

EMOTIONS AND DESIGN FOR OPTIMISTIC FOCUS

Next, let's apply these strategies further to build out your best overall creative strategy.

What emotions and actions should you tactically embed in your marketing to generate the feeling that makes the most sense for the regulatory state your consumers are in?

Some emotions to evoke in promotion regulatory creative are:

- Optimism
- Praise
- Nurturance
- Love
- Admiration
- Happiness
- Joy
- Excitement

In the actual marketing design for an optimistic focus, you would show people being praised, working quickly, and considering a lot of alternatives (because these consumers are open to new opportunities). You'd maybe show creativity, novelty, and innovation as well.

People with a promotion focus value advancement, change, and progress. They have a rosy outlook about the success of your product, and they want to feel happy. You should show luxury, comfort, and sophistication.

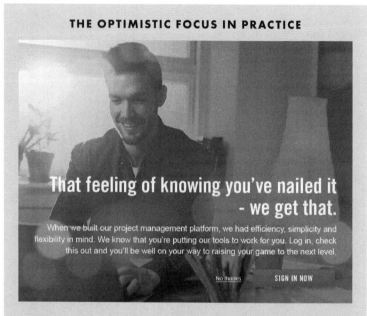

THE OPTIMISTIC FOCUS IN PRACTICE

That feeling of knowing you've nailed it - we get that.

When we built our project management platform, we had efficiency, simplicity and flexibility in mind. We know that you're putting our tools to work for you. Log in, check this out and you'll be well on your way to raising your game to the next level.

No thanks   SIGN IN NOW

Look at this image. Notice how it shows a single person to signal independence. And his happy, confident expression is showcasing a moment of achievement. His active posture only serves to hammer home the fact that he is accomplishing something significant.

Moreover, the copy also primes an optimistic approach. The words *built*, *efficiency*, and *raising your game* all signal ego validation, which triggers feelings of pride and happiness.

EMOTIONS AND DESIGN FOR CAUTIOUS FOCUS

Emotions to evoke in prevention regulatory creative include:

- Security
- Conservatism
- Safety
- Calmness
- Familiarity
- Tradition
- Stability
- Pessimism
- Caution
- Relief

In cautious-focused marketing pieces, you could show people being criticized. You could show the looming possibility of failure. Or you could show people making plans and being thorough, careful, thoughtful, accurate, and harmonious.

Cautious-focused people want to work slowly and deliberately. They want to feel prepared. They stick to tried-and-true behaviors and products that feel safe. These people also want to feel less worried and less stressed. They value conformity, tradition, and security.

Eliminate the risk of missing a payment by streamlining your billing system.

Our project management platform has been engineered from the ground up with security, flexibility and simplicity in mind. One try and you'll learn what thousands of customers already know - project management is one step closer to worry-free.

No thanks   SIGN IN NOW

Notice how the visuals prime the reader for caution. By including multiple people, the ad signals interdependence. Also, the model is looking directly into the camera with reserved posture (crossed arms) and a worry-free expression. She looks secure and protected.

The copy focuses on risk avoidance with the words *engineered*, *security*, and *worry-free*. It also triggers your desire for conformity by reinforcing that thousands of customers also use this product.

EXAMPLES: NIKE VERSUS UNDER ARMOUR

Let's assume that people who buy Nike or Under Armour products are under the achievement motivation. You could debate that, but it's probably true.

Look at Nike, which I think is most commonly a promotion/optimistic brand, based on what you see in their activation. You have a professional athlete with his arms stretched out wide. He's screaming. He's looking above the camera. The outstretched arms and emotion of rage are promotion primes.

Then there's the tag line: "Just do it."

Source: telegraph.co.uk

Contrast that campaign with Under Armour's. The focus is on a different professional athlete. You see him, arms at his sides, looking directly into the camera. Then you see the word *protect*. That's a cautious cue. The campaign is talking to consumers with a prevention/cautious approach to category decisions.

Both brands do a great job of communicating this: "We will make you an achiever." But depending on the consumer's regulatory focus at the time, one approach will work better than the other.

The ads might *look* similar to a consumer, but the

consumer won't *feel* the same. If the consumer has a cautious-focused regulatory fit, they'll likely be drawn more to the Under Armour ad.

Source: behance.net

While some people, E. Tory Higgins included, say that you can successfully message to both focuses, my experience shows that choosing only one approach is the best choice. As a marketer, I'd encourage you in most cases to make the decision one way or the other.

And it may not be easy, but you can always change your targeted focus. I had that conversation last year with a *Fortune 500* pet food brand. It was a tough conversation because they'd been talking to their consumers in an optimistic way for the past *thirty years.*

I understand that it can be a controversial decision to change the feel of a major brand. "I get it," I told them. "It's a hard decision. But that's why you're brand managers."

It's not always easy to change, but it's easier than the alternative.

I hear all the time from marketers who tell me they don't want to be a cautious-focused brand. "That's not us," they'll say. "We're an optimistic brand."

"Cool," I'll reply. "But we did the research, and your *customers* want you to be focused on helping them avoid risks or loss. So just know that every time you talk to somebody in an optimistic way, you're effectively messaging against their instincts."

HOW TO IDENTIFY REGULATORY FOCUS

So now that you know the importance of identifying your consumers' regulatory focus, how do you actually do it?

Here are the techniques we most commonly use in our behavioral research studies toward assessing someone's regulatory focus in that category. In all these techniques, look for the previously described strategies and emotions in the phrasing of their responses. These are *tells* that tip off their true approach when making decisions.

STORYTELLING AND FILL-IN-THE-BLANK EXERCISES

Similar to the questions we ask to identify goals, we ask consumers to tell us about the first time they ever used the brand. Then we ask follow-up questions such as, "What was going on? How did the brand help you reach your goal? How does it now?"

COLLAGES

And as I mentioned before, we have people build collages. When they build collages and talk about them, they may use words such as *secure* (signals cautious focus) or *innovative* (signals optimistic focus). A consumer's collage, and the story they tell with it, will definitely help you understand their focus.

INDIVIDUAL IMAGES

We've also used a proprietary battery of optimistic and cautious images, available for consumers to freely choose from. We have them select images that feel intuitively right to them, as it relates to a purchase decision. We ask them to choose images that make them feel as though they want to talk more about them.

WHAT'S THE FINAL STEP?

After we capture consumers' responses, we then analyze and sort them into optimistic versus cautious piles. We'll eventually see the trend and be able to make the overall classification.

Did someone use fifteen examples of optimistic language and only four examples of cautious language? Great. Now you know that they generally approach the category with an optimistic focus.

You rarely see 100 percent of someone's responses in one approach. But if the research comes back as half optimistic and half cautious and you're a new brand, you can just pick the focus that is the best fit for your brand. If you're launching a new brand and the brand doesn't stand for anything yet, there's no existing messaging to be incongruent with.

If you have to choose a focus for a new brand and you have no consumer research, I'd recommend using a promotion, or optimistic, messaging strategy in your marketing copy. With an innovative, new-to-the-world product, it helps to have the consumer in an aspirational mindstate, thinking about the upsides of using the product.

On the other hand, tried-and-true brands such as Coca-Cola and Kellogg's have a large share of their category. Large brands like these would most often benefit from trying to prevent their shoppers trying new products and thus lean toward using a prevention, or cautious, messaging strategy.

Now that you understand how to frame your brand's benefits, it's time to take a look into the fourth and final piece of the Mindstate Behavioral Model—triggering consumers' *behavior*.

CHAPTER 7

TRIGGER THE BEHAVIOR

Consider this: when people are in a state of high emotional arousal, they're more susceptible to influence. That's technically why emotional marketing works.

Once you have somebody in that state, you need to understand how to make it intuitive and easy for them to make a decision. In this chapter, you'll learn how to accomplish that through the powerful influence of behavioral economics and triggers.

MENTAL SHORTCUTS

Consumer decisions are very often driven by mental shortcuts, or triggers. And I should know—I was triggered into making a poor choice for one of the biggest decisions of my life.

As I was finishing my master's degree at Texas A&M University in 1997, I needed to decide what path to take for my career. Those were the dot-com days—a bullish economy where everybody seemed to have jobs and job offers that included pet benefits too!

I needed to choose one of four options. I had three job offers for marketing research positions in Cincinnati, San Antonio, or South Florida. The fourth option would be to forgo all the jobs and work on my PhD at my alma mater in Gainesville, Florida.

In trying to decide which option was best, I thought about both the jobs *and* the cities I'd be living in. *Do I know people in Cincinnati? Whom do I know in San Antonio? How many people even live there?*

I visited each city. I picked apart each job in every way

imaginable. I tried to do cost-benefit analysis across the four different life-changing places I could start my career.

It was an overwhelming amount of information to take in. My brain was overloaded with questions, considerations, and data. It was exciting and frightening at the same time. Making a choice felt *impossible.*

In these types of situations, our brains help us out by using mental shortcuts known as cognitive heuristics to make decisions easy to make. And these triggers have a large influence on our daily experience and broader lives.

I grew up in West Palm Beach, Florida, close to where one of my job offers was located. I was triggered into thinking, *Well, if I take the job in South Florida, I'll know people there. I know the roads and the restaurants. This feels like the better path for me.*

I chose the position in Florida even though it paid much less than the job in San Antonio. I made that decision because it was the *simpler* one. West Palm Beach was familiar, and without realizing it, that familiarity became the lead factor in my ultimate decision on how to begin my career. I found myself justifying taking less money for a position with less growth potential and rationalized myself into choosing an obviously inferior job. Only later did I fully understand that I was heavily influenced by a trigger called familiarity effect.

When people are in moments of high emotional arousal, like I was with my career decision, they will likely use cognitive heuristics without knowing it to help them make their decision. In my case, that led me to prefer the option that felt more familiar to me, and it therefore felt like the simplest and best path to take.

COGNITIVE HEURISTICS ARE EVERYWHERE

On a daily basis, these triggers help us make hundreds of decisions. But how exactly does that happen?

Let's hop into a Yellow Cab taxi and chat about it.

Before 2010, New York City taxi drivers were earning tips of 10 percent on average. You'd tell the driver where to take you, he'd get you to your destination, and you'd give him the fare plus a modest tip in the form of cash.

But then something happened. Almost overnight, the tip percentage more than *doubled* for New York City taxi drivers. Why did this happen?

Was it a booming economy? Nope, we were still in the middle of the Great Recession.

Did the taxi drivers take a customer service training program? No, they all had the same terrible service they always do.

Did the taxi companies set up an ad campaign to tip drivers better? Absolutely not.

The real answer was much simpler. The taxi companies put *credit card readers* in their cabs.

When it came to tipping the driver at the end of the ride, the new credit card readers highlighted three choices on the screen, in this order:

- A 15 percent tip
- A 20 percent tip
- A 25 percent tip

Now, let's be honest. The vast majority of people can't easily calculate a 15 percent tip on a $13.00 fare and make change. (It's a lot of effort!) But you know what isn't a lot of effort? Selecting the middle tip option out of three that are presented on a digital screen. Here's why: with the driver right there in front of you, you often feel uncomfortable choosing the lowest amount (I mean, the guy is right there!), and most would agree that a 25 percent tip for a New York City taxi driver is a bit excessive.

So what do you do? You do what is mentally easiest and deemed fair. You simply hit the middle button. *That's* why tips doubled overnight. It wasn't because of a slick advertising campaign, and it wasn't by convincing passengers that taxi drivers were now worthy of this level of a tip. And it wasn't a result of building an emotional connection with these drivers either. It was a simple matter of using a behavioral trigger to set up a really smart choice architecture that made higher tipping mentally easy for passengers. And it just so happened to be double the normal tip. Now, that's behavior design.

Instinctively choosing the middle option reflects the power of cognitive heuristics. They are quick mental shortcuts used by everyone to make decisions easier. It's not the highest tip amount. It's not the lowest amount. It's the middle option. Thanks to cognitive heuristics, the middle option often feels like the safest, best decision.

But why? What exactly are these cognitive heuristics, and how do they actually drive decision-making?

In this chapter, we'll answer those questions. We'll also explore how to use these triggers to your advantage as a marketer. But first, let's go back to where cognitive heuristics have been extensively studied for their role in human decision making—behavioral economics.

WHAT EXACTLY IS BEHAVIORAL ECONOMICS?

Behavioral economics explains the effects of psychological, social, cognitive, and emotional factors on decision-making. While the term *behavioral economics* implies that this only applies to economic decisions, the industry's research and findings extend well beyond economics. It actually extends into *all* decision-making.

Behavioral economics is still relatively young. Although in existence since the 1970s, the field was only recently popularized in the 2000s, after gaining great credibility and importance through the work of Dan Ariely, Robert Cialdini, Ravi Dhar, Daniel Kahneman, and Richard Thaler. Kahneman and Thaler both won Nobel Prizes in Economics for their work in behavioral economics, and many great books have been written on the subject. I have a list of my favorite behavioral economics books to read (in order), podcasts, blogs and events you can attend to learn more on my website mindstategroup.com/resources.

For the purposes of this book—*Marketing to Mindstates*—we'll look at behavioral economics as a framework to make all decisions *easy* and *intuitive* for people who are triggered into a state of high emotional arousal, or what is sometimes referred to as a psychological "hot state."

Cognitive heuristics completes the fourth stage of the Mindstate Behavioral Model. So far, we've learned how to activate a consumer's goal, we've primed their motivation, and we've framed their choice in a way that matches their regulatory fit and focus. At this point, we should have triggered a psychological hot state in our customer, and they want to act. It's the moment of psychological influence called a trigger point.

Now it's time to use the power of behavioral economics to make their action easy, intuitive, and immediate. How do we do that? By triggering actual behaviors using *cognitive heuristics*—mental shortcuts.

Creating high emotional arousal isn't enough on its own. As marketers, we've all seen consumers who engage with our product for several minutes, and they're clearly going to buy it. But they don't. They overthink the decision, put it down, and walk away.

If you incorporate cognitive heuristics to capitalize on feelings of high emotional arousal, you'll be *much* more likely to get consumers to take actions they would not have taken otherwise because you made that action mentally easy. Heuristics can be thought of as the bridge that links emotional hot states to actual behaviors.

WHAT ARE HEURISTICS?

Think of cognitive heuristics as rules of thumb, or triggers, that we all use to make decisions faster and easier.

Triggers help people simplify decision-making by eliminating the need to conduct cost-benefit analyses for every decision. Instead, we can simply use a decision shortcut we've learned to make it easy.

The impact that triggers have on us are often outside our consciousness. As consumers, we don't realize we're using them or that we're under their influence while in these hot states. Yet we *need* them, which is why we use them multiple times every single day. To successfully make the 35,000 daily decisions our brains need to make, we use these heuristics—time-saving mental shortcuts that have worked for us at some point in the past—just to be able to get through the day.

WHAT'S AN EXAMPLE OF A HEURISTIC?

There are many types of cognitive heuristics, and we'll take a quick look at the most common ones that we see that affect most consumers (and should therefore be incorporated into your marketing). But to give you a quick example, here are two of the most common cognitive heuristics in the United States—*scarcity effect* and *loss aversion*.

- **Scarcity effect** is our predisposition to place more value on things perceived as being scarce or limited. That extra perceived value can trigger some to act in the moment. That's why we're more likely to buy—and buy right *now*—when we see the words "Only ten seats left!" on an airline's website.

- **Loss aversion** is our predisposition to overemphasize the value of things that we own (or things that we *perceive* we own). When under this triggered influence, we seek to avoid losing things we feel ownership over. That's why we can find it so hard to sell our favorite bicycle or recliner or walk away from anything we feel psychological ownership over, such as a club membership.

THREE THINGS TO KNOW ABOUT HEURISTICS

Heuristics are commonly used, they're universal, and they're systematically and repeatedly used to make decisions. Let me explain further.

THEY'RE COMMONLY USED

Heuristics are the most dominant cognitive device used to make decisions today. Why? Because, again, we now have 35,000 decisions to make every day. We're heavily reliant on System 1 thinking and heuristics to make the vast majority of our daily decisions. Our daily lives are heavily influenced by these heuristics.

THEY'RE UNIVERSAL

Regardless of nationality, age, religion, gender, or any other demographic classification, we all use these heuristics to make decisions. A forty-year-old in Japan is just as susceptible to using a heuristic to decide on what to order at a restaurant as a teenager in the United States.

THEY'RE SYSTEMATIC

We often use the same heuristic over and over again. In fact, we'll use a heuristic repeatedly to subconsciously make decisions, until the point when it stops working in our favor. Unfortunately for most people, we're rarely aware of that point in time when a cognitive heuristic turns into a *bias* that can lead to bad decisions.

For example, *social proof* and *conformity effect* are common heuristics that can get people into trouble. Conforming to an in-group is important, especially to a teenager. They're trying to build their self-identity and figure out their role in a broader group. Teenagers look at what other teens are doing (social proof that "everyone is doing it") and then conform to the group they want to be most associated with.

The problem is that the more they conform, the more likely it is that they're making the same negative choices and bad behaviors as the broader group members. They may start drinking or smoking pot just to be part of the group, for example.

When negative effects start to appear—perhaps an

expensive ticket from a police officer for being a minor in possession of alcohol—the teenager may realize that social proof has steered them away from the decisions they want to make. They might realize that being like the crowd isn't working for them and they want to break free of making decisions based on social proof and conformity.

That's just one example of how people do the same thing over and over until something negative happens and snaps the use of that heuristic. But social proof will continue to affect people in different contexts, such as ordering a dish in a restaurant after being told it's the most popular.

HOW HEURISTICS INFORM CREATIVE

When you know the heuristics your target consumers use to make decisions in your category, you can then embed these triggers into your messaging to bypass people's need for conscious, critical thinking.

You're helping people think *less*. You're making the decision easier for them to make.

Anytime you get the opportunity to help people engage with a product *emotionally*—instead of thinking logically about it—that's a better proposition for you as a marketer. People take actions that are emotionally compelling, not *cognitively* compelling.

THE TOP TWENTY-ONE HEURISTICS TO TRIGGER

To identify your customers' decision heuristics used in your category or service, you'll need to know the most common heuristics to look for when people describe their purchase journey. There are more heuristics than we'll discuss here, but I've narrowed the list to the twenty-one most universal and impactful heuristics that we see again and again when it comes to studying subconscious mindstates.

A quick note on the terminology. I refer to a heuristic as the mental shortcut itself, neutral in terms of its result (good decision or bad decision). I refer to a heuristic as a bias when the mental shortcut has become problematic (i.e., results in bad decisions).

Here are the heuristics, or triggers, arranged alphabetically, so you can refer to them quickly in the future.

Like our other previous concepts, I am purposefully describing these in layperson's terms so we don't get bogged down in psychological jargon. If you want more depth on any of these or other heuristics, I'd encourage you to visit behavioraleconomics.com and download any of their behavioral economics guides for free. Alain Samson has done a great job pulling together the very best thinking in this area.

1. AMBIGUITY EFFECT

The ambiguity effect is our predisposition to avoid unclear options and unknown outcomes. We will often avoid products and services that seem hard to use or have unclear benefits or details.

Unless you're the brand leader in a category, you don't want to make your product or service feel difficult in any way. Similarly, you want to make your message as clear and simple as possible. Sometimes that means you need to not waste the consumers' time with all the product elements, specifications, and benefits that seem important (but aren't).

2. ANCHORING

Anchoring is our predisposition for one option (normally the first option) to be used in measuring all other options. Without that heuristic, people would look at every element as its own unique, independent reason for choice. But with this heuristic, a decision is anchored by one option.

Grocery "endcaps" are a common example of this. Shoppers often see the discounted price of a product on an endcap in a grocery store and then use that price to evaluate the pricing (and perceived value) of other, sometimes unrelated items in an aisle.

As a marketer, one way to use anchoring to your advantage is to do everything you can to become the anchor.

Be the first option. Be the first product customers see in a store aisle or the first thing that comes up on an Amazon list.

3. ATTENTIONAL BIAS (OR LIKABILITY EFFECT)

Attentional bias (or likability effect) is the predisposition for our perceptions to be affected by recurring thoughts. The idea is that people see and pay attention to things that are more top-of-mind.

This is why after you buy a new car, you tend to see it much more often than you had before. Attentional bias is what breaks through the clutter (all the other cars on the road) and makes you notice one particular type of car.

4. AVAILABILITY BIAS

Availability bias is our predisposition to overestimate the likelihood of an event that has recently happened because it is more available in our memory, regardless of the facts.

After a major airplane crash, people tend to believe airplane crashes are more likely to occur than what statistically is probable. This is because the event is more top-of-mind and readily available in memory. Therefore, some will irrationally switch to driving long-distance trips instead of flying, even though traveling by car is statistically far more dangerous than traveling by plane.

5. CONFIRMATION BIAS

Confirmation bias is our predisposition to search for, interpret, and remember information that confirms our current opinions or beliefs. This is often referred to as confirmation *bias,* because it's commonly used to describe mistakes made when using this heuristic.

Using this heuristic, people gravitate to information, products, and services that reconfirm their opinions and beliefs (and therefore their self-identity).

6. CONFORMITY EFFECT

The conformity effect is our predisposition to match attitudes, beliefs, and behaviors to "people like us" to conform to the broader group because it feels like a safer, easier, or more ideal option. The conformity effect keeps people from having to figure out acceptable behaviors in social settings. It's a copycat effect.

People often match their views and behaviors to what they perceive others expect of them. This is why we dress up for weddings or church. It's why we're quiet in elevators and libraries.

7. DECOY EFFECT

The decoy effect is our predisposition to modify the preference between two options by introducing a third one that leans toward one of the original two.

Let's say you're preparing two monthly TV subscription plans. You can get forty channels for $40. Or you can get eighty channels for $80. In this scenario, many people would choose the lower-cost option. It's a price-based value.

But you can sway value perceptions toward the higher-cost option by offering a third option, such as ninety channels at the higher-still price of $150. When people compare all three, suddenly the middle option looks more appealing and the lowest-cost option looks less so.

8. EGOCENTRIC BIAS

The egocentric bias is our predisposition to believe that positive results come from our individual actions, not from chance or another outside influence.

People like to feel they're due all the credit for reaching their goals. People want to feel as if they're in control of their destiny and that their choices are the reason they're successful. This can easily digress into an egocentric bias.

To market effectively into this heuristic, focus less on your brand's benefits and more on giving credit to your buyers. Most brands would be better off by not talking about their product's benefits but instead celebrating their consumers' actions.

9. HALO EFFECT

The halo effect is our predisposition to let the positive or negative feelings about one entity spill over, or halo, onto another nearby entity.

When someone at a party tells a funny joke, a listener tends to like that person, regardless of the joke teller's true character. In the same way, when people like one element of a product or brand, they generally like all the elements of that product or brand.

If your brand's direct mail piece is explaining all the advantages of an insurance policy, you should put your logo next to those benefits. Perhaps it says, "You can save $400 a year. You will get the best access to doctors. It's simple and easy to sign up." Those are positive things. Put your logo close to those benefits, and the positive associations that people have to those benefits can *halo* to the brand.

10. HYPERBOLIC DISCOUNTING (OR IMMEDIACY BIAS)

Hyperbolic discounting (or immediacy bias) is our predisposition to value an immediate payoff over a later one even if the later one is much bigger.

Hyperbolic discounting helps to explain why people use coupons they find on cereal packages more than they use those of even greater value sent to their home. They buy a box of cookies only for the instant reward of peeling the fifty-cent discount coupon off the package. That coupon seems more compelling in the moment than the dollar discount coupon waiting at home.

11. IKEA EFFECT

The IKEA effect is our predisposition to place a dispro-portionately high value on objects we feel part of creating. When people buy furniture from IKEA, they generally need to assemble it themselves and value it more as a result.

This effect happens regardless of the quality of the result. Even if it's a piece of furniture that looks terrible, the con-sumer will value it more highly because she took the time and effort to put it together.

When Betty Crocker originally launched as a cake mix, all you had to do with it to make cake batter was add water. The brand had dismal sales when it originally launched in the market, and at first, nobody could figure out why.

Then they found out that the mix took too much of the effort away from consumers, who wanted that experience and feeling of effort required to make their family a "homemade" cake.

So the brand removed the eggs, adding an additional step for consumers: add water *and two eggs*. That's all it took. The consumers felt better about the product when they contributed more to the process. The cake mix took off.

12. IN-GROUP BIAS

The in-group bias is our predisposition to give other people *preferential treatment* when those people are perceived to be similar to ourselves.

When people buy weight-loss products, they look for testimonials from people with an age that is close to their own or a weight that is (or was) close to their own weight. That similarity makes the consumers feel more comfortable making the purchase, because they perceive it to mean they can achieve the same results.

13. LOSS AVERSION

Loss aversion, again, is our predisposition to overemphasize the value of things that are personally owned or *perceived* to be owned and the desire to avoid losing those things.

What's an example of using loss aversion in marketing? A credit card offer that reads, "You are prequalified for this exclusive offer." That signals to consumers that they already own it and they'll lose it if they don't sign up.

14. MENTAL ACCOUNTING (OR LICENSING EFFECT)

Mental accounting (or licensing effect) is our predisposition to categorize options into mental buckets and find balance among those buckets to make our choices easier.

People often modify behaviors to keep an overall balance among the buckets. A successful dieter often evaluates food that way to limit the consumption of bad foods. In trying to balance good and bad decisions, they might justify their decisions to give up on their diet over the weekend. *I ate well all week, so I deserve a treat today*, they might think.

That's the idea of mental accounting. Similarly, it comes into play at the grocery store. If a consumer has filled their cart or basket with vegetables, fruits, and healthy foods, it makes it easier to add less healthy foods. *I've got so much good stuff here that it's OK for me to indulge a little*, they might think. *I can't have my kid eat only sticks and grass, right? Let me just go down the cookie aisle.*

I often tell brands, "Don't try to be a 'better-for-you' cookie. You're competing against all the healthful things in the grocery store and in the consumer's shopping cart. So don't claim to be healthier. You need to go the *opposite* way. Talk about how *indulgent* your cookie is, because in this category, that's what cookie shoppers are looking for."

15. PEAK-END RULE

The peak-end rule is our predisposition to evaluate an entire experience by its most positive or negative peak and also how it ended.

When people come back from vacation, they'll often describe the entire trip to their friends based on its best or worst moments, or their feeling on the final day. That approach is much easier that evaluating the vacation's merits day by day and hour by hour.

As a marketer, then, you make one or two things incredibly cool and exciting because a consistent experience is less memorable than one with one or two peaks. Even if the whole two weeks of vacation were enjoyable, those peak moments or the very end are the most important.

It's also the way people talk about movies. They talk about the action-packed battle scene or the surprise ending. They don't say, "Well, first let me introduce the characters." Instead, they say, "Oh my God, it had this kickass car crash, and then the hero wins!"

As a brand, you should be amplifying those peak moments and the memorable ending.

16. PRIMACY EFFECT

The primacy effect is our predisposition to remember the end points of any list versus items in the middle.

For example, car shoppers who look at a lot of different options most often go with the first and last cars they looked at when they're making comparisons or choices. Every option in the middle kind of blends in together. To influence the decision, then, try to be the first or last product customers see.

While preparing for a campaign presentation or a brand pitch, attempt to be the last agency to present. Your second choice should be to go first. Either way, never choose to go in the middle, because this heuristic often makes it harder for you to differentiate yourself.

17. RECIPROCITY

Reciprocity is our predisposition to be reciprocal in nature. If somebody feels you did something for them, there's often a desire to do something for you in return. It's a social contract that we all feel.

That's why when you're at a bar and somebody buys a round of beers for everybody, you feel such a strong desire to buy the next round. In marketing, this is most often used in sampling products at the retailer. After you've been given some free food at the grocery store, this heuristic might drive you to feel like you should buy something in return to reciprocate.

18. SCARCITY EFFECT

As mentioned earlier, the scarcity effect is our predisposition to place greater value on things perceived to be limited or scarce.

People often buy items in a grocery store that limit the number they can buy ("Limit five per customer!") or limit the amount of time they have to buy them ("Offer expires today!").

19. SOCIAL PROOF (OR THE BANDWAGON EFFECT)

Social proof (or the bandwagon effect) is our predisposition to do or believe things that we perceive are popular among others.

In marketing, consumers are more likely to buy services identified as "our most popular option." They perceive safety in buying things that are more universally appealing. McDonald's boasts "over a billion served" as social proof because it emphasizes quantity. (Conformity effect, by contrast, would emphasize that fellow buyers are "people like you.")

20. STATUS QUO BIAS

The status quo bias is our predisposition to like things that remain the same. People are often creatures of habit. They don't tend to like change.

This is why so many people choose the same brands again and again. Often, product loyalty is assumed to be driven by emotional connection, when the truth is it's just as often driven by the status quo heuristic. It's the desire to avoid change and save the time it would take to consider new options. They don't want to think about every decision every time.

This is where many brands make huge mistakes. They mistakenly believe they need to make constant improvement or changes to maintain consumers' loyalty. But even though changing the packaging or the flavor might actually benefit the consumer, it can backfire. Changes force consumers to change a habit. People know how to find their tried-and-true brands by their design cues. A design change to the packaging could cause them to reconsider your brand and, in doing so, consider your competitors for the first time in years.

21. SUNK COST FALLACY

The sunk cost fallacy is our predisposition to continue an action despite evidence that the action is a bad or inferior choice.

The classic example is a person's reluctance to leave a movie theater early, even though they really dislike the movie. People often keep watching because they've already "sunk" the cost, both time and money, into the decision to go there in the first place.

In marketing, you can use this heuristic to your advantage by helping people feel committed to an action or process. Salespeople call this the "foot-in-the-door" bias. They want to get you to commit to something small first, such as allowing them to step into your home or coming over to the car dealership. "Why don't you just come out and test-drive the car? You don't have to buy it, of course."

When people commit to anything and take more actions toward it, they're more likely to accept future commitments. They're often unable to view their previous actions (and expenditures) as the sunk costs that they are.

HOW DO HEURISTICS DRIVE BEHAVIOR CHANGE?

Again, your job as a marketer is to use messaging and experiences to increase your consumers' emotional arousal, and you need to do that. But most importantly, you need to engage them in a way that triggers an actual *behavior*. You need to get somebody to *act* differently.

That's where heuristics come in. Heuristics trigger consumers to act *now* rather than thinking through a cost-benefit analysis to make a decision. They help nudge people to move from emotional arousal to actual *decision-making and action*.

And that's why it's important to incorporate a heuristic (or two or three) into your messaging when they are in these trigger points.

And don't just use any heuristics; incorporate only the ones your consumers use in the moment of decision and match back to their subconscious mindstate, even if it's in just one sentence of your message. That may be all that's needed to move them to action when they're in their key mindstate.

Using the right heuristic at the right moment makes

decision-making feel natural to people. When you identify the top two or three heuristics your customers use in that key moment (in context) then you can incorporate that into your marketing to trigger action.

EXAMPLES OF HEURISTIC-INFLUENCED MARKETING

If you know your target consumers are influenced by the action of others (in other words, social proof) when making purchases in your category, you use that in your marketing. Recommendations or callouts can remind consumers that thousands or millions of other people have used this product. Or even take it a bit further: "Thousands of people have trusted us. You should too."

If you know reciprocity is important to your shoppers, maybe explore the use of sampling programs or giving free items to potential customers. This is at least part of Costco's success as a whole. When customers get nine or ten samples of food for free, there's a building sense that Costco gave them something, and shoppers feel the need to buy things in return.

That's one important reason why sampling works so well. It's built on an important and powerful cognitive heuristic.

You can factor in anchoring when determining your pricing. Research your consumers shopping in a grocery store or on your website. What's the first price they see? Can you control that "anchor" price? You definitely want to, if you can, because that's how people are going to measure the value of your brand and your pricing. No judgment or evaluation of a price is made without something to anchor it to. If you control that anchor, you can control how your price is judged.

HOW TO IDENTIFY HEURISTICS IN RESEARCH

I cannot overestimate the importance of identifying the top heuristics your consumers use when making evaluations and decisions. Therefore, it is critical to do all that you can to uncover them by engaging consumers with this in mind. If you *really* want to identify people's cognitive heuristics, get them to tell you stories—from beginning to end—about using your product. If you listen closely and read a little between the lines, you'll easily be able to identify the mental shortcuts that were influential in their decision to buy (or not buy) your product.

You could ask a shopper why she chose to buy the new Greek yogurt, for instance. And she might say, "You know what? I heard about it from my mother-in-law. She said her friends at her bridge club were talking about how good it is."

Bam! That's social proof. Now you know other people and their experiences influenced her.

But there's often more than one heuristic in play, which is why you want to hear the full story from beginning to end. The shopper might continue with, "Also, as I was walking in, they had free samples." That could be signaling the power of reciprocity being felt at the store.

You can also ask this very open question: "What was important to you when you first bought this type of yogurt?" By leaving a blank, people sometimes will say something like, "It was important to me to know that other people also had bought this yogurt."

As the consumer continues to talk about her purchase, keep following up with open-ended questions. I like to ask, "Why did you do that?" or "What was most important in that moment?" If you'll do that for each key trigger point in their decision journey, they'll give you more and more detail and at least one heuristic—but possibly several.

WHAT HAPPENS NEXT?

After the interviews, we look at the consumers' replies and deeper comments through the lens of each of these top twenty-one heuristics. It's through those verbatim responses that we'll be able to uncover which heuristics are most commonly used in the decision-making for our category or brand.

In many cases, we'll be able to narrow it down to the top three heuristics used. Next, we play around with different ways to align our future creative with each heuristic. You may not need to use all three, and you should use good judgment, because messaging for too many heuristics can make your marketing feel disjointed and cluttered. Then we'll test each of them in separate executions until one emerges as the best. Often, it's also the one that feels intuitive to our creative consultants.

The option that feels most natural is usually the one you should be using anyway. Net: go with your gut here. If you've spent any time in the business, you'll intuitively know what to do.

NEXT STEPS

Now that we've covered the four elements of the Mindstate Behavioral Model—goals, motivations, approach, and cognitive heuristics—it's time to use these insights to identify the most important factor of all—your consumers' *mindstate.*

PART THREE

APPLYING THE MINDSTATE BEHAVIORAL MODEL TO MARKETING

CHAPTER 8

APPLYING THE MINDSTATE BEHAVIORAL MODEL

You've now learned the primary aspects of the Mindstate Behavioral Model. You've learned your target consumers' goals and motivations. You've learned their regulatory approach, and you've identified the cognitive heuristics they use in their decision-making.

Applying the Mindstate Behavioral Model can be analogous to planning a long road trip for your customer. You've determined where they want to go by uncovering their goals. The motivations you've discovered for your customers provide the engine driving them forward. Their regulatory approach serves as their guiding light, or GPS, down the road, and they even found some thinking shortcuts to use along the way in the form of heuristics.

The next step is to use the four parts of the Mindstate Behavioral Model to influence your target consumer at the moment of decision—by marketing specifically to their subconscious mindstate in that moment.

These temporary mindstates significantly influence (and even override) people's normal attitudes, beliefs, and behaviors in moments of decision. This is why people often make decisions that seem irrational—eating dough-nuts despite being on a diet, buying the latest gadget despite being broke, or buying a new brand despite being satisfied with the brand they usually buy.

For every moment in your life when you acted in oppo-sition to what you thought was right, or acted without really thinking about it, there was an explanation for it. It wasn't because you suddenly formed a new preference. It's not because you stopped liking your past choices or became disloyal to your favorite brand. And it definitely isn't because you were convinced that this was a better choice. Here's the thing: when you act on impulse or instinct, nine times out of ten it's being driven by a tem-porary mindstate you're under in the moment. And if you think about how often you and your customers do this daily, you'll soon learn that the opportunity to market to these mindstates is enormous.

WHY IT WORKS (AND RESULTS I'VE SEEN)

When you integrate all four factors from the Mindstate Behavioral Model into your messaging and creative, it will directly tap into your consumers' subconscious.

Your marketing *will* be effective and *will* influence behavior.

I *know* this works. After conducting hundreds of behavior research projects, I've seen firsthand the power of marketing to people's subconscious mindstates.

Your research and marketing solutions become *significantly* more effective when they're designed around the behavioral principles we've covered so far. Most importantly, when you use behavior design effectively in your creative, you'll see powerful results in driving consumer behavior, consumer engagement, and most importantly, consistent topline sales growth.

Here are some quick examples of the results we've produced from using behavior design to market to people's mindstates:

- Doubled coupon redemptions for a global beverage manufacturer
- Optimized the online experience for a large financial services company
- Increased variety-seeking behaviors in restaurants
- Optimized the total customer experience in a large home improvement store
- Increased brand preferences in grocery aisles
- Increased cross-purchases for product manufacturers
- Optimized product innovation globally
- Lowered customer call volume in a large financial services company
- Optimized packaging design for some of the world's biggest brands
- Increased email response by four times

Science-based marketing creative drives *real* results in *real* business.

Let's move on to the final steps you need to take to identify and market to your consumers' mindstates and achieve the same types of results for your brand.

HOW DOES IT ALL WORK?

Once you identify and deeply understand the key subconscious goals, motivations, regulatory approach, and cognitive heuristics used by your target consumers in key trigger points, you'll have everything you need to identify the specific mindstate you'll be targeting with your marketing.

The four forces of the Mindstate Behavioral Model combine to form eighteen different mindstates. Once you've identified your target consumer's decision-making mindstate, you can then reference a specific mindstate *persona* and marketing *blueprint* for that mindstate (which we'll cover in the next chapter).

This unique mindstate blueprint will direct your overall behavior-design strategy and provide *specific tactical guidelines* for your marketing and messaging moving forward. These personas and blueprints were built to be practical and easy to implement today.

First, let's take a more detailed look into mindstates and how they're organized into persona overlays and marketing blueprints.

ELEMENTS OF A MINDSTATE

Again, a mindstate is a temporary state of mind when a person shifts from rational to *emotionally intuitive* decision-making.

Consumers in these emotional hot states are *much* more

susceptible to influence because they're relying on that System 1 subconscious processing of information (and subconscious decision-making). When a consumer makes decisions within that mindstate, that decision-making process is effortless and immediate.

If you're able to trigger them into that mindstate, you'll be better able to influence them, and they'll be more receptive to your marketing. But to do that, you'll need to know the core components of a mindstate.

A mindstate is the combination of two core components of our behavioral model: people's regulatory approach to decision-making (optimistic versus cautious) and the core motivation that's driving behavior in these moments.

You've learned that there are nine core motivations and two regulatory approaches. This results in eighteen different combinations (and therefore eighteen different mindstates).

Here's an example of two of the eighteen mindstates. These two have the same motivation but different regulatory approaches:

- **Optimistic Achievement mindstate.** Consumer is driven by the core motivation of achievement and has a *promotion* regulatory focus.

- **Cautious Achievement mindstate.** Consumer is also driven by the core motivation of achievement but has a *prevention* focus.

So to identify which of the eighteen mindstates are most important to build your persona and creative strategy around, all you need to do is identify their core motivation and their main regulatory approach. That's it!

For example, after your research, you may determine that a large group of your customers are driven by achievement motivations, and their main regulatory approach is optimistic. You can now feel confident that this group is under the influence of the Optimistic Achievement mindstate when making decisions in your category.

Alternatively, another group of your customers may be driven by the belonging motivation, and their main regulatory approach is cautious. Therefore, this second group is under the influence of the cautious belonging mindstate when making decisions in your category.

Next, with these mindstates identified, you'll use a specific mindstate *profile* to better understand your consumers' subconscious mindstate in the moment of decision-making. The profile should also guide the strategic *and* tactical considerations you need to integrate into your messaging to make it psychologically more effective.

WHAT'S A MINDSTATE PROFILE?

Each of the eighteen different mindstates has its own unique profile and specific tactics to use in future marketing. This is a psychological profile of what is happening in a consumer's mind in the moment of consideration or choice. To be clear, this is *not* a personality type. This is an "in-the-moment state of mind" influencing people's attitudes, beliefs, behaviors, and yes, even personality.

Therefore, each mindstate profile helps you understand and design marketing creative for that consumer's conscious and subconscious decision making.

Think of a mindstate profile as an extra layer of psychological comprehension that helps you better understand and drive consumer behavior. It helps you discover why your customers *really* do what they do. Every brand knows its target consumer. A mindstate profile is an explanation of why your customers don't always behave according to their beliefs and attitudes. It adds to, rather than replaces, what you already know about your customer.

With a mindstate profile, you'll be able to understand customers' psychological characteristics, behavioral goals, motivations, and how they approach their goals in the moment.

You'll be able to answer these questions: What are the

specific feelings and emotions they want to feel when they're in these mindstates? What are the top cognitive heuristics we should incorporate into our messaging to make customers' decisions easier?

Additionally, each mindstate profile includes a persona overlay and marketing blueprint that gives you a practical guide proven to optimize your marketing for this unique mindstate. These blueprints will direct you in establishing your brand's role in the consumer's life and also the *consumer's* role in the decision to choose your brand.

Most importantly, these marketing blueprints contain very specific tactical guidelines to help you scientifically *influence* decision-making.

So what exactly is in each mindstate profile?

MINDSTATE MARKETING PROFILE OVERVIEW

A Mindstate Marketing profile is composed of (1) a mindstate persona that can be used in conjunction with your current persona understanding, and (2) a marketing blueprint that takes you from deep mindstate understanding through an overall content strategy, content tactics and even ideation tools to reach this mindstate. These blueprints move your creative teams from persona understanding to specific behavior design strategy and tactics.

MINDSTATE MARKETING PERSONA

Mindstate Personas are designed to provide you with the tools to deeply understand and empathize with this customer at the moment of a decision. Without deep empathy, your marketing and business will always feel disingenuous and slightly off to your customers, so it's important to start all creative endeavors with these overlays. Persona overlays are composed of six parts.

MINDSTATE PERSONA OVERVIEW

If you have only thirty seconds to talk to somebody in a particular mindstate, the overview gives you a quick sense of who the person is in this moment. It helps you build emotional and behavioral empathy with your consumer in these hot state moments, and more importantly, it establishes a behavioral strategy to create messaging around.

MINDSTATE PERSONA OVERLAY

The mindstate persona overlay helps add to your understanding of what's happening psychologically with that person in this moment. The characteristics help you develop greater empathy and understanding of consumers in particular mindstates and help you understand what's influencing their attitudes, beliefs, and behaviors at the moment of decision.

Characteristics constitute things like:

- What do they desire from a brand?
- What do they value in that moment?
- What do they believe in that moment?
- How are they most likely to behave when they're in this mindstate?
- What brand and other preferences are they likely to have as it relates to the messaging?

GOAL TO ACTIVATE

When you activate consumers' higher-order goals, it brings those goals to their minds and provides direction to act. To make your messaging more salient and meaningful in key decision moments, brainstorm creative ways to activate on their aspirations and higher-order goals.

MOTIVATION TO PRIME

The next step is brainstorming creative ways to identify and prime the motivation—consumers' implicit emotional desires to pursue a goal. Again, motivation is the engine that drives people to go after their goal.

APPROACH TO FRAME

When you understand whether a consumer approaches

decision-making with an optimistic (promotion) regulatory focus or a cautious (prevention) regulatory focus, you can psychologically frame your brand, product, or service to fit their subconscious decision-making.

TRIGGERS TO CONSIDER

In this section of the mindstate profile, you'll see the cognitive heuristics that are most likely to be used in the moment of decision and therefore incorporated into your messaging. Remember, cognitive heuristics make decision-making easier for consumers. If you've never done this type of research, this section of the profile will tell you the top heuristics to consider marketing to right out of the gate.

Then you can brainstorm ways to use heuristics to bypass people's needs for critical thinking and effort while they make decisions. You'll eliminate their need for cost-benefit analysis. You'll make their choice feel more intuitive.

Typically, four or five heuristics (at most) apply to each mindstate. They're the ones that can be most attractive and useful to a consumer who has been triggered into that particular mindstate.

MINDSTATE MARKETING BLUEPRINT OVERVIEW

While the previous sections of the profile are focused on understanding consumers in this mindstate via a persona, this section focuses on the content strategy needed to drive your marketing tactics.

A Mindstate Marketing blueprint is composed of three parts that guide you from deep mindstate understanding, through an overall content strategy, content tactics, and even ideation tools to reach this mindstate. These blueprints move your creative teams from persona understanding to specific behavior design strategy and tactics.

FEELINGS TO EVOKE

This is an important section of the profile detailing the specific feelings that are likely to be felt (or desired) by a consumer in a particular mindstate. Knowing which feelings to evoke will help your marketing creative increase emotional engagement with consumers (starting with the visuals, then moving on to the copy).

There might be up to seven distinct feelings that can be used to tap into a specific mindstate and relate to a particular motivation, for instance. This is important to understand. Emotions and motivations go hand in hand. If you stray outside of the ones listed in your profile, the marketing has the high potential of simply not feeling right to the consumer. It will feel a little bit off and is less likely to create the emotional arousal needed to trigger the behavior and action you want the consumer to take.

CONTENT STRATEGY

While the previous sections of the profile are focused on understanding consumers in this mindstate, this section focuses on the content strategy needed to drive your marketing tactics.

You'll use this part of the mindstate profile to understand how your consumers see themselves and how they see your brand's role in their lives at the moment of decision. Understanding both of these elements helps you avoid being too focused on your brand and not focused enough on how your brand fits into consumers' complex, busy lives.

CONTENT TACTICS

In this section, you'll see actual tactical considerations to use when designing visuals and copy that increase customers' emotional arousal and drive decision-making. You can use these tactics (and brainstorm similar ones) to market to consumers in this particular mindstate. You can also use these tactics to trigger consumers *into* an ideal mindstate.

In the actual mindstate blueprints, you'll see several tactics that will help you view future creative through the lens of behavioral science when evaluating creative in the future. I'm not suggesting that you should attempt to use every one of them (I don't think you even could!) Instead, you can simply use this section to think things through when brainstorming your own tactics. You can ask yourself, "Are we using these types of tactics in our execution?"

If you're not, question why you're not. You may have good reasons, and that's fine. But either way, it's a good idea to pressure test your creative against this. If you're not doing anything similar to the content tactics listed in the mindstate profile, then you're not fully optimizing your creative for consumers in that specific mindstate.

THE EIGHTEEN MINDSTATES

Here are the names of the eighteen unique mindstates. You can turn to the appendix of the book to read a brief synopsis of each mindstate profile.

1. Optimistic Achievement
2. Optimistic Autonomy
3. Optimistic Belonging
4. Optimistic Competence
5. Optimistic Empowerment

6. Optimistic Engagement

7. Optimistic Esteem

8. Optimistic Nurturance

9. Optimistic Security

10. Cautious Achievement

11. Cautious Autonomy

12. Cautious Belonging

13. Cautious Competence

14. Cautious Empowerment

15. Cautious Engagement

16. Cautious Esteem

17. Cautious Nurturance

18. Cautious Security

NEXT STEPS

Now that we've introduced the key elements of these Mindstate Personas and the blueprints themselves, it's time to learn how to apply them into your marketing creative.

You're now ready to *market to mindstates*.

CHAPTER 9

MARKETING TO MINDSTATES

Now you're ready to move from theory to *action*. You're ready to use behavior design strategy to *drive* new behaviors using Mindstate Marketing.

As marketers, we know the importance of linking behavioral science and creative to optimize marketing. You need to trigger mindstates and intuitive decisions within them, using heuristics to make action immediate and effortless for your consumers, whether it's clicking a link in an email, making an impulse buy on a website, or switching brand loyalty.

With the Mindstate Behavioral Model and the eighteen mindstate profiles, you can be prescriptive in the tactics you use to increase your messaging's influence.

Using these mindstate profiles to drive creative strategy and tactics helps you have much richer, science-based conversations about your creative strategy and executions. You no longer need to make decisions based on subjective opinions.

Let's take a look at how your creative could change based on a mindstate profile. Imagine that you have determined that you should use the Optimistic Achievement profile because your customer is driven by achievement motivations and because their main regulatory approach is optimistic. Below are just a few of the strategic and tactical considerations you will find in a full mindstate profile and should consider using to activate this mindstate.

- Look for strategies to help customers *achieve their goal as quickly as possible*, even if that means adding risk.
- Evoke feelings of determination, success, accomplishment, and closure.
- Portray your customers successfully overcoming barriers to achieve their goal by *showing past successes* and how your product or service *enabled* it.
- Emphasize change, taking chances, innovation, and *seizing opportunity to win*.
- Show independence of the customer and how the solution contributes to their success.
- Show determined, confident expressions, particularly

when *overcoming a barrier to success.* Consider images such as breaking through the ribbon in a marathon.

- Pose model *to face away from the camera,* which makes the reader/audience a witness to the moment of success and achievement.
- Utilize *abstract, slightly unfocused backgrounds* with broader visuals of the product and moment of success.

Now let's contrast that with the behavior design tactics for someone in the Cautious Belonging mindstate. Below are just a few of the strategic and tactical considerations you will find in a mindstate profile and should consider using to activate this mindstate.

- Look for strategies to help customers *establish and maintain social relationships* by *eliminating barriers* to commonalities or camaraderie.
- Evoke feelings of inclusion, acceptance, connection, and unity.
- Portray your customers actively working to *eliminate division or disharmony* with others and portray your brand as being a key resource that *"in the future"* will *decrease their chance of not fitting in* or not being accepted.
- Emphasize stability, accuracy, and control in *being able to bond with others.*
- Show *collaboration with others working together* to

become closer and how the solution contributes to their ability to find acceptance or alignment.

- Show respected, peaceful expressions, particularly when another faces a lack of support.
- Pose model to *face directly into the camera to make eye contact with the reader*, which draws the viewer into the moment of inclusion by others.
- Utilize *in-focus visuals with simple, clean backgrounds* with close-up visuals of the product and moment of inclusion.

As you can see from the example above, your behavior design strategy and tactics will change quite a bit based on the mindstate your customer is under in the moment of decision.

THE SCIENCE BEHIND THE ART

We recently worked with a very large hotel group, and they had a problem. They wanted professionals to consider their hotels for business travel. After our research to identify these travelers' key mindstates they were under when deciding on business travel, we developed a series of behaviorally designed executions to drive brand penetration. One of the ads caught the eye of the chief marketing officer because of our decision to have the lead figure in the ad, a smiling business traveler, look straight into the camera.

The CMO asked us to explain why we made the ad look the way it did, and if our choices would be a turnoff for people of the opposite gender because they couldn't "see themselves" in the ad. Rather than explaining that the woman looked like one of their brand loyalists or focusing on diversity in the people or providing benefits in the copy, I instead had a science-based explanation for our choices.

The model facing directly outward toward the ad reader was placed there to trigger reciprocity. Likewise, because her pupils were dilated and facing outward, the reader of that ad may pick up a deliberate subconscious cue for increased interest in the reader, and they would reciprocate that interest in the ad and halo that to the brand.

The CMO said it was the best creative discussion they'd had in years. And that was because we had science backing our answers.

The only remaining step is to communicate in a way that builds your brand's story and equity.

HOW TO MARKET TO MINDSTATES

First, conduct marketing research with your target consumers, or use your intuition if you must, to identify and understand their goals. Again, you want to understand both the *functional* and *higher-order, aspirational* goals, asking:

- What goals are they trying to reach?
- Why are those goals important to them?

Next, determine the motivations and approach they use. Ask yourself:

- Which of the nine core human motivations are likely driving them to go after their goals?
- Are they approaching their goals through the lens of optimism or caution?

Once you have those questions answered, you'll be able to identify the most appropriate mindstate to build your strategy around. Next, identify which one or two of the eighteen mindstate profiles should be *focused* on and review the brief description of it in the appendix of this book.

FINAL STEPS: DEVELOPING CREATIVE

Now that you understand your consumers' mindstate, you can begin to develop your creative and messaging using the Mindstate Marketing profile that fits best with your customer. Each page in the profile will tell you exactly how to use that specific information in your marketing creative briefing, development, and evaluations.

With your creative team, brainstorm ways to activate consumers' aspirational goal through your brand. If you're offering a new product, ask, "How can we communicate that our new product will help this person reach their aspirational goal? To become the person they dream of becoming with the help of our brand?"

You want to empower your creative team by making sure they have these mindstate profiles in hand. Ask them to be aware of the profiles, but also to just do what they normally do—be creative. Be compelling. Find that nugget—that spark of passion you have around this idea—

and work from there, because that's where great creative comes from.

Then, once the team has come up with an idea, pressure test it against the targeted mindstate profile to make sure it generally aligns. Ask yourself and your team, "Are we still in the right place?"

You can use this test to decide whether to improve your creative ideas or throw them out entirely. For instance, if you need to speak to the Optimistic Achievement mindstate and your creative idea is the polar opposite of that mindstate, there's no sense in refining the idea any further.

But in many cases, your ideas will be moving in the right direction. You can then use your mindstate profile to *refine* those ideas to make them much more effective psychologically.

In the first stage of creative, use the mindstate profile to *evaluate* your creative.

Do it again in the second stage. Pressure test your marketing creative against the last parts of your Mindstate Marketing blueprint.

The marketing blueprints are particularly important

when you get to the *content tactics* stage. At this stage, you're starting to think about the creative visuals. You're thinking about the exact copy you'll use to set up a video or build into a print campaign or ad.

You want to make *sure* your tactics map back to the mindstate profile.

Again, don't *start* your creative from the mindstate profile and move forward from there. Start with your inspiration and ideas, and create a campaign that intuitively feels right for your brand. *Then* use the mindstate blueprint, mapping all creative ideas and tactics back to that.

The pressure tests will serve as a guide as you go through the creative process and get down to tactical execution.

What's an example of this? If you're marketing to a mindstate of belonging, and your creative isn't showing multiple people interacting with some level of commonality in the messaging and visuals, that's a red flag. Belongingness is hard to communicate without showing multiple people who look aligned and fully accepted by the broader group. If you show only one person, realize it's harder to get somebody to feel that motivation if you're not showing them interacting with others. Or if you're marketing to a nurturance mindstate, it's important to show people in close proximity, particularly face-to-face.

That's how a mindstate profile can serve as the guardrail.

Finally, when there's conflict between the behavioral strategy and brand equity, have tough conversations and make tough decisions. Realize that for every time you move away from behavioral activation, you risk losing customers.

Why? Because you risk losing true *emotional engagement*. And that's my number one focus. Make *sure* you have strong emotional engagement—emotional engagement that is *scientifically* designed to influence consumer behavior.

And if you do that, consumers will naturally and intuitively choose your brand.

CONCLUSION

Now that you've made it to the end of the book, you're in a position to better understand and influence consumer behavior. And that's a good thing, because if you're in any kind of marketing or sales role, understanding and influencing behavior is your *job*.

It's also the greatest job in the world. It's an *important* job. It's a job where you can make a *huge* impact on your business.

And it's a job where you can *change* marketing as we know it. We can rid the world of emotionless creative that doesn't move the business. We can make marketing research and marketing the largest growth driver in the company and worthy of significant investment.

IT'S TIME FOR CHANGE

As marketers, it's time for us to change.

We *need* to integrate behavioral science into our marketing to break through people's subconscious filter. What we're doing now just isn't working like it used to. Data analytics won't get us to where we are truly influencing long-term behavioral change.

We need to behaviorally design marketing so that our customers won't turn away or skip our ads.

We need to provide simple, intuitive advertising that helps them make good decisions for themselves.

If you're in the field of consumer insights or marketing research, you need to be doing research that focuses on *both* System 1 and System 2 decision-making.

Our role goes beyond helping our brands build awareness and stronger equity to drive brand *consideration*. Your new role is to also use behavioral science and behavior design strategies to drive consumer *choice*—to drive topline growth.

Consumer *choice* leads to positive business outcomes. That might mean driving an initial purchase of your brand, driving repeat purchases, or attracting additional retailers. That's what drives money into the company. And that's what behavior design can do for your brand.

As insight professionals, you can now use the power of behavioral science and design to increase your personal value to an organization. You can become your company's *behavioral change agent*. And it's only through the power of behavioral research and behavior design that this vision is possible.

And here's the great news: as marketers and researchers, we are best equipped to do this because we study human behavior every day! It's what we do. It's in our DNA. And most importantly, there's *nobody* more qualified than we are to own this role in business. You do something nobody else gets to do. You are blessed to study human behavior every day of your life.

The future of marketing is a blend of art and science—use that to your advantage. People in companies across the world are building brands, but few are using behavioral science to speak to people on a deep, subconscious, System 1 level. You can.

You are now empowered to market to mindstates and become the most strategic asset in your company's growth. Every new dollar that gets added to your bottom line is the result of someone's behavior change. It's a result of your ideas and guidance.

And now there's nobody more qualified to become their company's behavioral change agent than you. Good luck, and do great things.

THANK YOU—AND A BONUS

Thank you for reading my book! Please reach out to me on LinkedIn, or at mindstategroup.com and let me know how your Mindstate Marketing journey is working for you. I'd love to hear your story!

I've posted some bonus resources for you at mindstategroup.com. These resources include:

- Information on our various programs and services to help you successfully apply Mindstate Marketing to your business
- A case study on the Wicked Crisps brand, which was a brand we created from scratch, using the Mindstate Marketing program
- A PDF download of a Mindstate Marketing blueprint, which contains a mindstate persona and a marketing blueprint to build content strategies and content tactics

- A weekly blog on the latest findings from behavioral psychology and marketing
- Various Mindstate Marketing resources including a list of our favorite books, blogs, companies, and podcasts to dig into if you want to learn more about Mindstate Marketing

Thank you again, and I wish you the very best as you become behavioral designers!

APPENDIX

THE EIGHTEEN MINDSTATE PROFILES

Before you read any of these mindstate profiles, I want to make an important note about this appendix. The following pages provide an overview, summary, and list of characteristics for each of the eighteen unique mindstate profiles that people are under when they make decisions. Full persona overlays and marketing blueprints can be gained by continuing your Mindstate Marketing journey with us. Check out our offerings at mindstategroup.com to see which is best for you.

First, let's look at the optimistic mindstates.

1. OPTIMISTIC ACHIEVEMENT

Optimistic Achievement is the combination of an

achievement motivation and an *optimistic* approach to decision-making.

SUMMARY OF MINDSTATE

Being successful in our life's activities is a constant goal that we all feel. Whether it's losing that last stubborn ten pounds by eating healthy or working hard to get that promotion at work, we all want to feel the sweet success of achievement. Striving to achieve and celebrate our short- and long-term goals is a healthy part of everyday life. The anticipation of setting goals and steps taken to obtain them are part of the Optimistic Achievement mindstate.

MINDSTATE CHARACTERISTICS

- **Driven** to achieve a sense of accomplishment by taking the necessary actions to achieve their goals. In this mindstate, people will look for strategies to help them achieve their goals as quickly as possible, even if that means adding risk.
- **Desire** to take chances and seize untapped opportunities that they feel will help them achieve their goal. Having a successful closure with reward is also highly desired.
- **Value** the feeling of accomplishment that comes from overcoming obstacles to reach the final reward. In this

mindstate, the process of winning is just as important as the final moment of success itself.

- **Believe** they're worthy and personally responsible for the outcomes of their efforts versus circumstance or luck. Therefore, brands and products are important but ancillary in the process of achieving their goals.
- **Behave** by looking for opportunity, working quickly, considering many alternatives, and seeking positive feedback to know they are on the right track for success.
- **Prefer** novel, innovative approaches/solutions that significantly increase their chance of success.

2. OPTIMISTIC AUTONOMY

Optimistic Autonomy is the combination of an *autonomy* motivation and an *optimistic* approach to decision-making.

SUMMARY OF MINDSTATE

In today's world where choices can feel overly restrictive, gaining the freedom to experience life on your terms is highly desired. As we gain life experiences, an underlying desire builds to have the freedom to express our personal style and preferences in the products, services, and experiences we buy. The satisfaction we feel when we are able to have this freedom is the basis of the Optimistic Autonomy mindstate.

- **Driven** to feel distinct by expressing their unique preferences. In this mindstate, people will look for strategies that provide customization when pursuing their goals, even if that means adding risk.
- **Desire** tools that help them get what they want, in the way they want, in the time and place they want it. Being unbounded to choose their own path or action is highly desired.
- **Value** the feeling of uniqueness and freedom that come from having the authority to personalize with unbounded choice. In this mindstate, affirming one's ability to act/customize in the ways one personally desires is highly valued.
- **Believe** in building/finding distinct, customizable experiences or outcomes for their seemingly unique needs. They believe that freedom and individuality come when they can act on their desires.
- **Behave** by looking for opportunities to gain greater freedom to customize, work quickly, consider many alternatives, and are open to new possibilities to gain more freedom.
- **Prefer** novel, innovative approaches and solutions that allow them to find or build the perfect solution for them.

3. OPTIMISTIC BELONGING

Optimistic Belonging is the combination of a *belonging* motivation and an *optimistic* approach to decision-making.

SUMMARY OF MINDSTATE

In today's world where positive, long-lasting relationships are increasingly difficult to build and maintain, finding ways to really connect with others is highly desired. This desire is often so powerful that people will go to great lengths to find connections with others to know they belong to something larger than themselves. The desire to connect and build relationships by finding similarities and joint passions with others is the basis of the Optimistic Belonging mindstate.

MINDSTATE CHARACTERISTICS

- **Driven** to feel accepted by others by finding similarities that maximize their chances of greater camaraderie and approval. When in this mindstate, people seek to validate their core sense of social acceptance through cohesiveness with a larger group.
- **Desire** tools that help them establish and maintain social relationships by finding ways to discover the common good and then promote common needs and/ or passions.
- **Value** the intrinsic feeling of community/connection

that comes from being liked and accepted by others or having shared interests that can be counted on when working together.

- **Believe** in developing deeper connection in their world to validate their sense of social acceptability.
- **Behave** by seeking social cues that help them predict their personal level of integration into a broader group and look for positive emotional expressions and physical actions from others that indicate their acceptance level.
- **Prefer** novel, innovative approaches and solutions that allow them to find or build a sense of community and/or expand their social connections with others.

4. OPTIMISTIC COMPETENCE

Optimistic Competence is the combination of a *competence* motivation and an *optimistic* approach to decision-making.

SUMMARY OF MINDSTATE

The importance of becoming our very best is something that we learn as children and take with us in our daily lives. Therefore, the feeling of becoming more proficient in an activity and the personal growth that comes with it is an important part of satisfying experiences. For many, the desire for competency can be best achieved by focusing our efforts on maximizing our chances of successfully reaching our pursuit of excellence. The desire to improve by doing our very best to maximize on our opportunities is the basis of the Optimistic Competence mindstate.

MINDSTATE CHARACTERISTICS

- **Driven** to feel competent in activities by maximizing on the opportunities to exceed their own personal standards. When in this mindstate, people seek to increase their expertise in an activity to validate their core sense of personal growth.
- **Desire** tools that help them explore and become more skilled in a passion by finding ways to improve their chances of overcoming barriers to improved proficiency. Allowing them to set, measure, and surpass their internal standards to perfect their skills is highly desired.
- **Value** the intrinsic feeling of constant improvement that comes from persistence and continued learning.
- **Believe** in building internal excellence through acquiring greater proficiency and qualifications. When pursuing goals, shortcuts and luck are not nearly as important to success as self-determination, perseverance, and grit.
- **Behave** by looking for opportunities to gain greater skill or competency, work quickly to find them, and consider various alternatives.

- **Prefer** novel, innovative approaches and solutions to how your solution will make them more capable.

5. OPTIMISTIC EMPOWERMENT

Optimistic Empowerment is the combination of an *empowerment* motivation and an *optimistic* approach to decision-making.

SUMMARY OF MINDSTATE

In today's world where choices and experiences feel overly restrictive, finding ways to gain greater control of one's experience is highly desired. This desire is a result of our drive to feel empowered—to feel capable and equipped to take on life's challenges. The desire to have greater control of one's life and choices is the basis of an Optimistic Empowerment mindstate.

MINDSTATE CHARACTERISTICS

- **Driven** to feel empowered by increasing their options and level of control in pursuing their goal. In this mindstate, people will look for strategies that help better equip them when pursuing their goals, even if that means adding risk.
- **Desire** tools that help them control important aspects of their situation to overcome challenges. Being

enabled and authorized to choose their own path or action is highly desired.

- **Value** the feeling of internal strength and pride that comes from rising to an occasion on their own. In this mindstate, affirming one's ability that they are empowered to meet an unreachable challenge is valued.
- **Believe** in the freedom needed to be in control of their final outcome. They believe that through control comes greater opportunity for success.
- **Behave** by looking for opportunities to gain greater access or control, work quickly to find them, consider various alternatives, and try options that they previously felt were limiting.
- **Prefer** novel, innovative approaches and solutions that allow them to figure things out and to be in charge of their options and path to success.

6. OPTIMISTIC ENGAGEMENT

Optimistic Engagement is the combination of an *engagement* motivation and an *optimistic* approach to decision-making.

SUMMARY OF MINDSTATE

Feeling pleasure and excitement in our life's activities is something we need daily. Whether it's losing ourselves in a new video game or tasting the perfect birthday cake that we've waited all day for, we all want to feel emotionally and physiologically engaged to bring a greater enjoyment to life. This desire to feel fully engaged in key moments and get the most stimulation out of products is a part of the Optimistic Engagement mindstate.

MINDSTATE CHARACTERISTICS

- **Driven** to feel that they are getting the most out of their product, service, or experience. In this mindstate, people will look for strategies that provide experiential ways of pursuing their goals.
- **Desire** tools that help them live the experience to the fullest, in a way that is fresh and absorbing. Being fully immersed and involved in the experience is highly desired.
- **Value** the feeling of emotional lift (or relaxation) that comes from having fully engrossing, sensory-based experiences. In this mindstate, balancing boredom and overstimulation across the entire experience is highly valued.
- **Believe** in the power of being fully engaged (or lost) in the moment by ongoing pulses of novelty and unpredictability to heighten the experience.
- **Behave** by looking for opportunities to get the most out of the moment by focusing on the product/service

and how it can help start and maintain pleasure or tranquility.

- **Prefer** novel, innovative approaches and solutions that allow them to increase and then hold their attention and pleasure/serenity throughout the experience.

7. OPTIMISTIC ESTEEM

Optimistic Esteem is the combination of an *esteem* motivation and an *optimistic* approach to decision-making.

SUMMARY OF MINDSTATE

In today's hypercompetitive, interconnected world, it is increasingly difficult to "rise above the crowd." Whether it's our post being liked on Facebook or being commended in front of our workmates, positive recognition is often our most alluring, secret desire. Feeling popular, for even the smallest reason, helps to build our ego and self-confidence. The desire to improve our chances of being publicly recognized and praised is the basis of the Optimistic Esteem mindstate.

MINDSTATE CHARACTERISTICS

- **Driven** to feel admired and valued in activities by maximizing the opportunities to be recognized socially. When in this mindstate, people seek to increase their noticeability and popularity.

- **Desire** tools or products that help them measure and improve their future social standing among others.
- **Value** the intrinsic feelings of acceptance and pride that come from flattery, renown, or fame.
- **Believe** in products or experiences that can be measured so as to validate/improve their social standing among others.
- **Behave** by looking for opportunities to gain greater popularity, consider various alternatives, and try new options that help them stand out from the crowd, even if risky.
- **Prefer** novel, innovative approaches and solutions to how your solution will make them more recognized and admired.

8. OPTIMISTIC NURTURANCE

Optimistic Nurturance is the combination of a *nurturance* motivation and an *optimistic* approach to decision-making.

SUMMARY OF MINDSTATE

Some of us view the world as needing greater compassion and love—a place where people are more empathetic, cared for, and supportive of each other. This behavioral mindset is a result of our deep desire to feel protected, supported, and appreciated by the ones we love in life. The feeling of pure appreciation and love is a part of the Optimistic Nurturance mindstate.

MINDSTATE CHARACTERISTICS

- **Driven** to achieve a sense of appreciation by providing care and support to others/themselves. When in this mindstate, people seek greater affiliation and cooperation, often in an attempt to feel greater trust.
- **Desire** to make others/themselves feel deserving by finding ways to increase opportunities and ways to show that they care or are able to "right a wrong."
- **Value** acts of consideration, thoughtfulness, and generosity, particularly to help reach a goal.
- **Believe** in being protective, supportive, and compassionate by showing love with tangible, physical action.
- **Behave** by working deliberately, have positive expectations, and seek positive feedback from actions. Preparing for future moments of care are also key actions taken when in this mindstate.
- **Prefer** ways to show short-term and longer-term nurturance so they are assured that they can provide/feel love over time.

9. OPTIMISTIC SECURITY

Optimistic Security is the combination of a *security* motivation and an *optimistic* approach to decision-making.

SUMMARY OF MINDSTATE

In today's chaotic world, finding ways to feel more secure is desired for almost all of us. We work every day to protect the people and things we have from loss or misuse. The relief we feel when we are free from worry is the basis of Optimistic Security.

MINDSTATE CHARACTERISTICS

- **Driven** to achieve a sense of security by maximizing their chance of making their future goal a reality. In this mindstate, people will look for strategies to help them achieve their goals in a way that has a good balance between risk now and reward in the future.
- **Desire** to focus on strong competencies that they feel will help them prepare to reach their goals. Having strong experience and expertise is highly desired, as are the trust and relief of knowing that every precaution has been taken to help them reduce barriers in reaching their goal.
- **Value** the feelings of inner peace and trust that come from having more predictability in reaching their goal. In this mindstate, stability and consistency during the

process of reaching their goal are key to the overall enjoyment of their experience.

- **Believe** that building predictable outcomes via expertise and tried-and-true processes is the best way to reach their goals. Therefore, brands and products that have established themselves as honest, transparent, and having a track record of success are significantly advantaged.
- **Behave** by looking for opportunity, working quickly, considering alternatives, and seeking reassurance that they are making good, consistent decisions.
- **Prefer** "second generation" innovation that has at least been tested to provide more predictable, safe outcomes.

Now let's review the cautious mindstates:

10. CAUTIOUS ACHIEVEMENT

Cautious Achievement is the combination of an *achievement* motivation and a *cautious* approach to decision-making.

SUMMARY OF MINDSTATE

Being successful in our life's activities is a constant goal that we all feel. Whether it's losing that last stubborn ten pounds by avoiding junk food or not missing that deadline to get that bonus at work, we all want to feel the sweet success of achievement. Striving to achieve and celebrate our short- and long-term goals is a healthy part of everyday life. The anticipation of reaching our goals by avoiding potential pitfalls is the basis of the Cautious Achievement mindstate.

MINDSTATE CHARACTERISTICS

- **Driven** to achieve a sense of accomplishment by avoiding mistakes that may cause them to not achieve their goals. When in this mindstate, people seek to avoid mistakes that could cause them to not succeed.
- **Desire** tools that help them reduce risk and avoid any possible barriers that could limit their ability to achieve their goals. Having success in their actions that lead to successful closure with reward is highly desired.
- **Value** the intrinsic feeling of accomplishment that comes from overcoming obstacles to reach the final reward. In this mindstate, the process of winning is just as valued as the success itself.
- **Believe** they're worthy and personally responsible for the outcomes of their efforts versus circumstance or luck. Brand solutions are important but ancillary in the process of achieving their goals.
- **Behave** by working slowly and deliberately in an effort to reduce risks and seek positive feedback to

know that they are on the right track to avoiding barriers to success.

- **Prefer** tried-and-true solutions with concrete reasons and examples of how your solution will bring them success in reaching their goals.

11. CAUTIOUS AUTONOMY

Cautious Autonomy is the combination of an *autonomy* motivation and a *cautious* approach to decision-making.

SUMMARY OF MINDSTATE

In today's world where choices can feel overly restrictive, finding ways to prevent a loss of self-autonomy and individual expression is highly desired. As we gain life experiences and individuality, we prefer freedoms that help us avoid conformity through the products, services, and experiences we buy. The satisfaction we feel when we avoid limitations in how we choose to reach our goals is the basis of the Cautious Autonomy mindstate.

MINDSTATE CHARACTERISTICS

- **Driven** to feel distinct by expressing their unique preferences to avoid restrictions to their freedom of choice. In this mindstate, people seek to avoid being restricted or controlled in their ability to reach their goal.

- **Desire** tools that help them get what they want, in the way they want, in the time and place they want it. Being unbounded to choose their own path or action is highly desired.
- **Value** the intrinsic feeling of uniqueness and freedom that comes from having self-determination. In this mindstate, affirming one's ability to act/customize their solutions in the ways they personally desire is highly valued.
- **Believe** in building/finding distinct, customizable experiences or outcomes for their seemingly unique needs. They believe that freedom and individuality come when they can act on their desires and avoiding controlled experiences is vital to success.
- **Behave** by working slowly and deliberately in an effort to avoid anything that could limit their freedom of self-determination.
- **Prefer** tried-and-true solutions with concrete reasons and examples of how your solution will allow them to find, build, or customize the perfect solution for them.

12. CAUTIOUS BELONGING

Cautious Belonging is the combination of a *belonging* motivation and a *cautious* approach to decision-making.

SUMMARY OF MINDSTATE

In today's world where positive, long-lasting relationships are increasingly difficult to build and maintain, finding ways to really connect with others is highly desired. This desire is often so powerful that people will go to great lengths to avoid potential disharmony. The desire to connect and build relationships by avoiding potential exclusion by others is the basis of the Cautious Belonging mindstate.

MINDSTATE CHARACTERISTICS

- **Driven** to feel accepted by others by avoiding mistakes that may cause them to be excluded by others. When in this mindstate, people seek to validate their core sense of social acceptance through avoiding repudiation by a larger group.
- **Desire** tools that help them establish and maintain social relationships by eliminating barriers to commonalities or camaraderie.
- **Value** the intrinsic feeling of community/connection that comes from not being disliked or rejected by others, or having shared interests that can be counted on when working together.
- **Believe** in developing deeper connections in their world to validate their sense of social acceptability.
- **Behave** by working slowly and deliberately in an effort to avoid things that could disrupt their social

acceptance. They look for negative emotional expressions and physical actions from others that indicate their level of possible disapproval by others.

- **Prefer** tried-and-true solutions with concrete reasons and examples of how your solution will help them avoid being shunned or ignored.

13. CAUTIOUS COMPETENCE

Cautious Competence is the combination of a *belonging* motivation and a *cautious* approach to decision-making.

SUMMARY OF MINDSTATE

The importance of becoming our very best is something that we learn as children and take with us in our daily lives. Therefore, the feeling of becoming more proficient in an activity and the personal growth that comes with it is an important part of satisfying experiences. For many, the desire for competency can be best achieved by focusing our efforts on minimizing mistakes in our pursuit of excellence. The desire to improve by doing our very best to avoid potential errors is the basis of the Cautious Competence mindstate.

MINDSTATE CHARACTERISTICS

- **Driven** to feel competent in activities by avoiding

mistakes that may cause them to not surpass their own personal standards. When in this mindstate, people seek to avoid decreases in their expertise in an activity, to validate their core sense of personal growth.

- **Desire** tools that help them explore and become more skilled in a passion by finding ways to avoid common mistakes or other barriers to improvement. Allowing them to set, measure, and avoid obstacles to setting new, higher standards is highly desired.
- **Value** the intrinsic feeling of constant improvement that comes from avoiding stagnation and lack of progress.
- **Believe** in building internal excellence through avoiding obstacles that would make them less proficient and qualified. When pursuing goals, shortcuts and luck are not nearly as important as self-determination and perseverance, to avoid mistakes.
- **Behave** by working slowly and deliberately in an effort to avoid things that could cause them the chance to lose proficiency.
- **Prefer** tried-and-true solutions with concrete reasons and examples of how your solution will make them avoid stagnation.

14. CAUTIOUS EMPOWERMENT

Cautious Empowerment is the combination of an

empowerment motivation and a *cautious* approach to decision-making.

SUMMARY OF MINDSTATE

In today's world where choices and experiences feel overly restrictive, finding ways to increase the ability to control one's experiences is highly desired. This desire is a result of our drive to feel empowered—to feel capable and equipped to take on life's challenges. The desire to avoid restrictions when making choices is the basis of the Cautious Empowerment mindstate.

MINDSTATE CHARACTERISTICS

- **Driven** to feel empowered by decreasing variability and lack of control in pursuing their goal. In this mindstate, people will look for strategies that help better equip them with the power needed to reach their goals.
- **Desire** tools that help them control important aspects of their situation to overcome unforeseeable challenges. Being enabled and authorized to choose their own path or action is highly desired.
- **Value** the intrinsic feeling of internal strength and pride that comes from rising to an occasion on their own.
- **Believe** in the freedom needed to not lose control of

their final outcome. They believe that through control comes a greater chance of not failing to reach their goal.

- **Behave** by working slowly and deliberately for opportunities, to lessen the number of uncontrollable factors.
- **Prefer** tried-and-true solutions with concrete reasons and examples of how your solution helps them take charge of their options to avoid weakness.

15. CAUTIOUS ENGAGEMENT

Cautious Engagement is the combination of an *engagement* motivation and a *cautious* approach to decision-making.

SUMMARY OF MINDSTATE

Avoiding the monotony of daily tasks to elevate everyday experiences is the hallmark of a happy life. Whether it's playing on the phone while waiting to be called in a doctor's office or choosing sushi over an uninspired sandwich for lunch, we all want a daily escape from the norm. This desire to feel fully engaged in key moments by avoiding boredom and tedium is a part of the Cautious Engagement mindstate.

MINDSTATE CHARACTERISTICS

- **Driven** to avoid mediocrity in the products, services, or experiences they buy. In this mindstate, people will look for strategies that provide more experiential ways to pursue their goals.
- **Desire** tools that help them avoid boring, ordinary experiences by making them fresh and absorbing. Being fully immersed and involved in the experience is highly desired.
- **Value** the feeling of emotional lift (or relaxation) that comes from having fully engrossing, sensory-based experiences. In this mindstate, balancing boredom and overstimulation across the entire experience is highly valued.
- **Believe** in the power of being fully engaged (or lost) in the moment by limiting stagnation and rudimentary events.
- **Behave** by working slowly and deliberately in an effort to avoid things that could limit their full engrossment of a product, service, or experience.
- **Prefer** tried-and-true solutions with concrete reasons and examples of how your solution will help them avoid dull, lifeless experiences.

16. CAUTIOUS ESTEEM

Cautious Esteem is the combination of an *esteem* motivation and a *cautious* approach to decision-making.

SUMMARY OF MINDSTATE

In today's hypercompetitive, interconnected world, it is increasingly difficult to keep from being marginalized. Whether it's our post being ignored on Facebook or not being celebrated for a job well done, many work tirelessly to not be overlooked. Feeling popular, for even the smallest reason, helps to build our ego and self-confidence. The desire to decrease our chances of being overlooked or disregarded by others is the basis of the Cautious Esteem mindstate.

MINDSTATE CHARACTERISTICS

- **Driven** to feel admired and valued in activities by minimizing their risks of being unrecognized socially. When in this mindstate, people seek to maintain their chance of being noticed or special.
- **Desire** tools or products that help them decrease their chance of losing future social standing among others.
- **Value** the intrinsic feeling of acceptance and pride that comes from flattery, renown, or fame.
- **Believe** in products or experiences that can be measured so as to validate/maintain their social standing among others.
- **Behave** by working slowly and deliberately in an effort to avoid things that could cause them to lose the admiration or respect of others.
- **Prefer** tried-and-true solutions with concrete reasons

and examples of how your solution will maintain their social status.

17. CAUTIOUS NURTURANCE

Cautious Nurturance is the combination of a *nurturance* motivation and a *cautious* approach to decision-making.

SUMMARY OF MINDSTATE

Some of us view the world as needing greater compassion and love—a place where people are more empathetic, cared for, and supportive of one another. This behavioral mindset is a result of our deep desire to feel protected, supported, and appreciated by the ones that we love in life. The feeling of pure appreciation and love is a part of the Cautious Nurturance mindstate.

MINDSTATE CHARACTERISTICS

- **Driven** to achieve a sense of appreciation by providing care and support to others/themselves. When in this mindstate, people seek greater affiliation and cooperation by limiting conflict, often in an attempt to feel greater peace and harmony.
- **Desire** to make others/themselves feel deserving by limiting the chances of not finding ways to show that they care or are able to "right a wrong."

- **Value** acts of consideration, thoughtfulness, and generosity, particularly to help reach a goal.
- **Believe** in being protective, supportive, and compassionate by showing love with tangible, physical action.
- **Behave** by working deliberately and seeking positive feedback from actions. Preparing for future moments of care are also key actions taken when in this mindstate.
- **Prefer** ways to show short- and longer-term nurturance so they are assured that they can provide/feel love over time.

18. CAUTIOUS SECURITY

Cautious Security is the combination of a *security* motivation and a *cautious* approach to decision-making.

SUMMARY OF MINDSTATE

In today's chaotic world, finding ways to feel more secure is desired by almost all of us. We work every day to protect the people and things we have from loss or misuse. The relief we feel when we are free from worry is the basis of the Cautious Security mindstate.

MINDSTATE CHARACTERISTICS

- **Driven** to achieve a sense of security by minimizing

their chance of making a mistake while pursuing their goals. In this mindstate, people will look for strategies to help them achieve their goals in a way that helps them mitigate risks now.

- **Desire** to focus on strong competencies that they feel will help them prepare to avoid risks. Having strong experience and expertise is highly desired, as are the trust and relief of knowing that every precaution has been taken to help them eliminate the threats from reaching their goal.

- **Value** the feeling of inner peace and trust that comes from having more predictability in reaching their goal. In this mindstate, specific plans and a detailed focus on monitoring for risk are key to the overall enjoyment of their experience.

- **Believe** that building predictable outcomes via expertise and tried-and-true processes are the best way to reach their goals. Therefore, brands and products that have established themselves as honest and transparent and have a track record of success are significantly advantaged.

- **Behave** by working slowly and deliberately in an effort to be as prepared as possible.

- **Prefer** tried-and-true solutions with concrete reasons and examples of how risk is avoided by using your product.

ACKNOWLEDGMENTS

I want to thank four people for making this book happen:

Stephen Springfield, who inspired me.

Pam Forbus, who empowered me.

Gandalf, formerly Chuckles, who enables me.

And most of all, my beautiful wife, Melanie, who undoubtedly believes in me. You are the reason behind everything I am and everything I do. I love you.

ABOUT THE
AUTHOR

WILL LEACH is the founder and CEO of the Mindstate Group. The Mindstate Group provides behavioral science-based tools and resources to help you build consistently effective marketing creative and experiences that drives people to listen, care, and act. Will is also the founder and CEO of TriggerPoint, a leading behavioral research and marketing consultancy.

Will has over 25 years of behavioral insights experience, including running PepsiCo's behavioral research lab, and is an instructor at the Cox School of Business BLC at Southern Methodist University and Texas A&M's Human Behavior Lab. Will is also a two-time winner of the EXPLORE Award for behavior science research innovation and writes for national publications on the power of behavioral science in sales and marketing.

Will is an expert in using behavioral psychology to optimize marketing and experiences and is a frequent contributor to Forbes, writing about behavioral economics and behavioral marketing.

Visit his website at mindstategroup.com to learn about the many Mindstate training programs and other upcoming mindstate resources.

Made in the USA
Monee, IL
06 July 2023